UNDER THREAT
OF DEATH

UNDER THREAT OF DEATH

A MOTHER'S

FAITH

IN THE FACE

OF INJUSTICE,

IMPRISONMENT,

AND PERSECUTION

SHAGUFTA KAUSAR
WITH EUGENE BACH

WHITAKER
HOUSE

UNDER THREAT OF DEATH
A Mother's Faith in the Face of Injustice, Imprisonment, and Persecution

Eugene Bach
BacktoJerusalem.com

ISBN: 979-8-88769-235-7
eBook ISBN: 979-8-88769-234-0
Printed in the United States of America
© 2024 by Back to Jerusalem, Inc.

Whitaker House
1030 Hunt Valley Circle
New Kensington, PA 15068
www.whitakerhouse.com

Library of Congress Control Number: (Pending)

1 2 3 4 5 6 7 8 9 10 11 **WH** 30 29 28 27 26 25 24

CONTENTS

A NOTE FROM THE CO-AUTHOR

Sitting in a small, cramped apartment in western Europe, I sat across from Shagufta drinking tea. She had only been out of prison for a few months and was still getting used to life outside of death row. I had been closely following her dramatic story in the news for years and never thought I would have the chance to meet her in person one day, let alone sit in her home and hear her tell me the story of her entire life.

From everything that I had read about her in the news, I thought I knew her life's story, but hearing it directly from her while drinking tea together made me realize that there was so much more that had never been revealed.

Shagufta is not the first person I have met to be sentenced to death for refusing to deny her faith, but she is the first from Pakistan to tell a story that goes much deeper than her own. She represents thousands of modern-day Christians who secretly suffer from Pakistan's deadly blasphemy laws. Those brutal laws are currently starting to spread to other nations around the world, and Shagufta's story opened my eyes to them. Her story is a wakeup call to all of us.

The biggest challenge in writing her story was translation. I was surprised that Shagufta didn't speak English, since she was sentenced to death for sending a blasphemous text—in English! In order to get her story, Shagufta's brother Joseph had to spend hours and hours sitting together with us, translating from Urdu to English and back to Urdu again.

Telling her story is not safe or easy. Even though she currently lives in an undisclosed location in Europe, she and her four children are constantly threatened from Muslim mercenaries who want to kill her.

For security reasons, brevity, and context, some names, places, and events have been changed, condensed, combined, or omitted. To bring clarity to certain aspects of Shagufta's story, several conversations, people, places, and experiences were added that did not actually happen but that do represent real events or situations. Some details, names, places, and people have also been added to the story to replace real events that might be a security risk to people if they were to be shared unchanged.

Shagufta admits that some of the details of different events are not clear in her memory and may be remembered differently by others who were involved. In this book she attempts to share to the best of her ability for the sake of the reader.

Therefore, with full disclosure, by adding these descriptions and explanations, I have attempted to explain Shagufta's story in the clearest and fullest way possible while keeping her and her family safe.

—Eugene Bach

1

WHAT HAVE WE DONE? PART 1

I never felt as spiritual as I did that day in the interrogation room. It was not the kind of spiritual that one longs to feel when praying at church, but it was the kind of spirituality that leaves one with a feeling of having exited reality and stepped into something that can only be described as less than tangible.

I was like a ghost. Not alive and not dead. Not dreaming and yet not awake.

"What have we done?" I screamed, forcing the words out with my eyes clenched closed. The smog of confusion mixed with desperation and fear reeked in the nostrils of my tormentor.

Those eyes! I will never forget those deep dark black eyes staring back at me with the hatred of a goblin. The sounds were peripheral, mushed and scrambled, but the memory of his eyes seared permanently into my brain.

Was he a man or a demon? I read of devils in the Bible, but never thought I would ever see one. Now I was face-to-face with one. I closed my eyes again, hoping to shake the sight of him from my mind. I was huddled in the corner of an interrogation room while my four children screamed, covering their ears with their hands and desperately hiding their eyes deep in my chest. Like me, they didn't want to acknowledge the visual reality of what was happening to us.

"What have we done?" I cried out again. "Please stop. I promise, we didn't say anything against Islam." My youngest had her hands wrapped around my neck and was pushing her face up into the saddle between my nape and shoulder.

I had no comfort to offer my children. Their father was hanging upside down from the ceiling, being beaten by the ghoul standing in front of me with flames of shimmering fire in his grip.

Shafqat, my husband, couldn't see or hear us. The intense pain made him momentarily blind and deaf as he endured each strike from the officer's weapon. They shouted commands at him and demanded that he repeat what they said, but he couldn't hear them. Neither could I. Every sound they made with their mouths was suppressed by the adrenaline pumping through our bodies. The fight-or-flight physiological response was automatic, and the walls prevented our flight while the police suppressed our ability to fight.

"Blasphemy! Blasphemy!" chanted the angry imam just outside the room. His traditional Punjabi knee-length cotton top swished over his loose trousers as he paced back and forth. The imam's grey vest strained to hold his portly upper body in place as he raised his fists in the air, goading the anger of the crowd gathered in the lobby of the police station. He walked in and out of the room where we were being interrogated with authority.

His loose-fitting *shalwar* pants or *payjamas* made a swishing sound that cut through the silence of the noise. The western word *pajama* comes from the Pakistani Urdu word *payjama*, meaning loose-fitting clothing for the legs.

The crowd repeated the chant, "Blasphemy! Blasphemy!"

I didn't know what the word meant. I was guilty of the negligent crime of only having a loose idea of what the word meant. All I knew was that it was really bad, bad enough for them to wish me dead. I knew that the crime of blasphemy had been enough to earn the death sentence for a poor mother named Asia Bibi a couple of years earlier. I vaguely remembered hearing her crime of blasphemy but wasn't sure what it exactly meant.

Whatever the crime of blasphemy was in their eyes, I didn't do it on purpose. "Please!" I begged, clinging to my children. "Please, we will do anything. Stop hitting my husband."

No one heard me. Only the man with the evil dark eyes acknowledged that I was even there. My pleas did more to anger the imam than appease him. The angry mob in the hallway grew larger and squeezed in like transported cattle. The mob's hatred grew, and their vicious malice invigorated our tormentor even more.

"Confess!" the guard said, while swinging a stiff black rubber rod at Shafqat's hip again. My husband winced with pain, prevented by gravity from wrapping up in the fetal position.

"Don't you dare touch me, you piece of swine!" the guard said, jumping back as Shafqat swung toward him. My husband was an unclean infidel. Touching him would have made the Muslim guard unclean. He had been taught from an early age in Pakistan that Christians were unclean, more unclean than the multiple sweat rings that had no doubt formed over a matter of weeks under the armpits on his drab khaki green uniform without being washed.

"Ptew!" The other guard spit on my husband, a common form of disgust shown toward Christians in Pakistan.

"*Allahu akbar!*" he screamed as he swung his black rubber club again.

"Blasphemy!" they yelled again from outside the room, echoing the shouts of the imam.

"How dare you insult the prophet Muhammad!"

"We didn't do anything," I screamed. "I swear it. We don't know what you are talking about!" I cried, bowing my head down and pushing my children underneath me as I moved my forehead to the ground.

"Liar! We have the text message!" the guard said. "Confess!"

My husband writhed in pain, grinding his teeth in anguish, but refused to confess.

"Confess!" the guard demanded with another strike to the hip bone, but again Shafqat would not utter a word.

Having been bound to a wheelchair since being shot in the back several years ago during a debt collection dispute, Shafqat's body hung uncontrollably upside down from the ceiling like a sack of potatoes. He was completely at their mercy. There was nothing he could do to retaliate or guard himself from the next blow, but still, he would not confess.

We had nothing to confess to. They were saying that I sent a blasphemous text, but I didn't know how to read or write, and I had never used a mobile phone. If they would have only listened, they would know that I was innocent.

"Is he going to confess?" the imam asked impatiently, as if he had a schedule that we were delaying.

The guard turned and looked at the imam and grimly shook his head.

Stomping into the room, he pointed at me while keeping eye contact with Shafqat. "See your wife?" he thundered, with foaming spittle building up in the corners of his dry lips while wagging his dark finger at me, "If you do not confess right now, we will strip your wife naked, force her to walk down the street, and let the men of this city have their way with her and then lynch her in front of your children. And I will make sure that you stay alive long enough to watch every moment of it."

An evil silence fell on the room, broken only by the cries of my four children clinging to me with every ounce of strength they had in their little bodies. My youngest daughter's legs quivered as she kept clawing with her feet to push herself deeper into my neck.

I stopped breathing. The room went blurry. Shafqat's eyes welled up and streaks of tears flowed around the far corners of his eyes and down the grimy sides of his forehead. His face contorted for the first time in a look of anguish that was different from the grimace that he showed while being tortured.

The guards had spent the entire evening torturing Shafqat with every method that they could imagine to get him to confess to blasphemy, but they had regulated themselves to his body. He had been punched, slapped, kicked, spat upon, hung upside down and beaten, but now they were leaving his body and moving to his heart.

I wanted to scream out, "Confess!" but my voice left my mortal body. Nothing seemed real. I desperately wanted to wake up from this nightmare, but I wasn't asleep. My spirit was too discombobulated to utter even the feeblest of whimpers.

The room froze. A spiritual chill crept into the room like a lazy breeze announcing the quiet presence of demonic immorality. The once animated men were now all waiting for Shafqat to say the words that would decide whether I would be stripped naked and forced to be paraded through the streets of Toba Tek Singh.

I could not answer for my husband, nor could I confess for myself. I was already guilty in their eyes; they just needed my husband to admit it. My fate was in his hands.

After a short pause and more tears, he shook his head, indicating that he could not confess.

"So, you will not confess?" the imam asked with an odious quiver in his stark inquisitive eyebrows. Then he slowly turned back and looked at the diabolical brood behind him as if he were about to throw them a piece of raw meat. They all knew what the look meant.

Immediately, I looked up and saw the guard with the deep dark black eyes staring back at me. His arms went limp and hung down at his sides as if to announce that he was resigning his duties with Shafqat and would now focus his attention on me.

He looked at the imam and the imam nodded at him, giving him permission to drag my children away from me and hand me over to the mob.

2

HUMBLE BEGINNINGS OF FAITH, FAMILY, AND SCHOOL

"Shagufta!" I could hear my mother calling after me, but I was already halfway down the road, running into the blackness of the morning dark toward St. Philip's church. It was too late to stop and turn around to see what she wanted, so I just kept running.

I couldn't see the dust shuffle up behind me as I ran, but I could hear the miniscule pebbles flipping out from under my sandals and I breathed the dry fine particles of the air in through my nostrils. The morning sun was projecting a soft magenta glow behind me.

I was the first one out on the path this morning. I knew that I was riling up all the dogs as I passed each home. Their barking voices were fresh from a night of rest. I knew every dog along the way by name. Most of the people in my village were related in one way or another, and dogs played an important role in each home.

More than pets, our village dogs were respected members of the community, guarding the home at night from strangers, protecting food from other animals, and alerting the family when visitors approached.

There was no guard dog better than our dog Jackey. I called him Jackey-Jackey. He had twice the name because he was twice the dog. Aside from my mother, Jackey-Jackey was my best friend. He was always the first to greet me in the morning on my way to church and would run with me all the way to the path that bordered our yard. When I crossed the imaginary border of our family's property, Jackey-Jackey would stop and chase his tail in circles as if to say goodbye to me. He could not leave our home to follow me because he had the duty of watching over our chickens, sheep, and cow.

Beside the tree, we had a jug of milk that Jackey-Jackey had been guarding all night. "Don't let anyone touch this milk, Jackey-Jackey. Do you understand?" I would say to him in a playful high-pitched voice that I only used with Jackey-Jackey.

Jackey-Jackey would bark and sit by the milk with his floppy pink tongue hanging to the left side of his mouth. He had a way of smiling back at me, not with his mouth, but with his eyes.

Jackey-Jackey made our family different from many other families in Pakistan. Muslims believed that dogs were unclean animals, and because of their religion, they can't touch them. If a Muslim walked by our home, they would cross to the other side of the path when they saw Jackey-Jackey walking toward them. I never thought much about it, except that it made Jackey-Jackey's job of protecting our home much easier.

St. Philip's Church was only a few hundred meters away from our house. Soon my siblings would be running to join me in prayer. I was the oldest and would help my mother with the school preparations for the other children. I left early for prayer so that I could return early.

It was just before six o'clock in the morning so I knew my other siblings would soon be coming.

I turned the corner into the church yard, slowing my run to a brisk walk. The small humble cross atop St. Philip's Church was an adequate representation of the structure itself. Mud, clay, and crooked wood kept the uneven, leaning rhomboid structure erect.

St. Philip's Church was shared by both the Catholics and Protestants in our village. To be honest, I was not aware of the difference. I simply prayed to the Jesus of the Bible, and I expected that He heard my prayers.

It was our family practice that we would pray at the church every morning. We never missed a morning. "We must thank God every day for all He has given us," my father would say. He did not come from a long line of Christians. He and his family had to sacrifice a lot to remain Christian when Pakistan split from India.

"We are surrounded by people who do not share our faith," he would remind us as children, "but it is important to never forget where we come from."

Many Christians in Pakistan are cultural Christians, meaning that the Christian faith has been passed down to them from generations of believers, but that was not the case in our family. Our great grandparents were not Christian; they were Hindu. My grandmother and her family were all Hindu. When Pakistan declared its independence from India, there were many families that were ripped apart, not knowing whether to settle on the Indian side of the border or the Pakistani side of the border.

My great grandfather and his wife fled in one direction and their extended family fled to the other. When they found themselves on the Pakistani side, it was too late to return to the other side. Our grandfather and his generation of Christian believers really suffered for their faith. From the beginning, they were hated by most Muslims around them.

Despite their hatred, my grandfather lived a long life and outlived many of those who despised him. He settled in a small village and helped build St. Philip's Church. He was one of the most joyous believers. He was always the first to the church every Sunday morning and opened the gates to allow the other believers in.

"Never take your faith in Jesus for granted," my father would remind me, and his words contributed to our faithful prayer as a family every morning before we started our day.

I dropped to my knees at the front of the church and began my daily prayers. I always prayed in the manner that my parents taught me. "Dear Lord, on this day, provide us with the food that we need to sustain our lives and the lives of the animals You have given to us. Allow my father and mother to find work that will help put bread on the table. I pray for the health of Mother and Father so they can do the work that You provide. Lead us and guide us this day."

"We need the Lord to lead us and guide us every day," my mother said when teaching me to pray at home with the family. Praying for food and a job for my parents was a top priority for us. We had to rely on the Lord for our daily bread, every day. Our resources were so meager that they were drained by day's end, so we had to rely on God's provision for the next. We trusted Him to provide. We prayed for the harvest. We prayed for our health to go and get the harvest. We prayed for customers that they would be willing to buy our produce from the harvest. We prayed that there would be food left to purchase in the market at the end of the day when we had money at the end of selling our harvest.

We could not survive one day without the Lord's provision. Every day required faith.

As I prayed, I could hear the clacking of sandals slapping the wooden floors coming into the church one by one. I knew the specific sound of a shuffle that separated one sibling from another. Just by listening to the sound of someone entering the church, I was able to discern if the newcomer was a member of my family or someone from the village. Our home only contained one single room that all nine members of my family lived in. One learns the sounds that each one makes when they walk around a small room when they have lived in such close proximity.

Some of the older members of the community would come and read their Bible during morning devotions, but because I was unable to read, I spent the entirety of my morning praying.

On my way back home in the morning light, I noticed a tree with a ribbon tied to it that I had missed while running past it in the dark. The ribbon indicated that our friends had just had a baby boy. I made a note in my head not to stop at that house for the next forty days, because it is believed to be bad luck if a childless woman casts her shadow upon a newborn baby.

When I arrived home, Jackey-Jackey was there, frantically wagging his tail to greet me. From the edge of our courtyard, I could already smell the popping oils that mother was using to fry the warm *paratha* that awaited us returning from morning prayers. I could see her standing diligently over the small fire in the corner of the outdoor kitchen. She had a technique of placing each piece of flat roti bread in a slight bed of warm oil so that it wouldn't burn, but it would cook inside. My mother had the rare talent of injecting both flavor and comfort in each flaky layer.

Her eyebrows were pensive as she exercised patience, hovering over each piece of flatbread. She loved feeding people. My mother looked younger than her age, as most women often do when they carry love and kindness long into their adulthood. She had a strong nature, proven by her hard work often displayed in the fields and clay mines, though it did not detract from the amiability and tenderness of her movements.

I often sat for hours admiring her long, thick black hair that shimmered with contours of the light whenever she put her hands through it. Even as it was frosted with strands of grey, its luster grew more enviable with time.

She looked up from her frying pan when I walked closer and gave me a quick, but occupied smile. Her skin was a lighter shade of brown and her face lit up every time she shared that smile. Her mouth was perfectly symmetrical and full tan lips naturally puckered out a little as did her round cheeks. She wore poor tattered clothing well and gave them dignity. Her poverty never detracted from her regal pose.

I couldn't find any irregularity in her face, hair, or the clothes she wore and had no doubt what made my father fall in love with her.

My father was seated on the ground beside my mother, having his morning paratha with chai. He had nothing better to do than look at her. The chickens were pecking around the rocks, keeping a close eye on their nemesis, Jackey-Jackey.

The courtyard around our simple single-room brick house was bubbling with life. I could hear the metal mugs clanging, ready to be filled with fresh chai. Every home was brewing with a mixture of sweet spicy fruit, rose petals, almonds, cloves, and hints of cardamom in their Punjabi black tea. The metal spatula hitting the pan as mother flipped the paratha rang in unison with the clanging bell of our prized family cow walking next to its calf. Our cow provided milk for our family every day, which was often added to the chai.

The random bleats of our kid goats added to the morning symphony. Our small courtyard was a miniature organic farm.

I went and sat on the ground beside my father and grabbed a piece of flatbread from the plate in front of me. One by one, my siblings trickled in in their blue and white school uniforms and sat together on the ground to enjoy our tea and flatbread as is the Punjabi custom.

"Okay, Shagufta," my mother said, exhaling aloud. She didn't say anything more to complete the thought. She didn't need to. We both knew that it was time for me to take my brother and sisters to school. I had been taking care of the children in my family for several years. I was the oldest in the family, and it was my responsibility to look after them.

"Nasarin," I shouted to my sister, who was about two years younger than me. "Get Asaf and Joseph. It's time to leave for school." Asaf and Joseph were two of my younger brothers. I had another sister Rachel and a brother Gasha, but they were too young for school.

Together we marched back to the church where we had spent the morning praying. Our school was in the church. In the second part of the day, the church pews transformed into desks to make up a simple classroom.

The parents in our village only earned an average of twenty-five Pakistani rupees or ten cents per day and did not have the money to send their children to great schools. Pakistani parents put high value on an education for their children, but unfortunately for too many, poverty and Islam held them back from achieving that goal.

One of the major benefits of being educated by the church was that students were not forced to study Islam. One of the downfalls was that much of the rules of Islam remained a mystery to me.

The teachers also worked for the church, so their dual employment kept the price of tuition down. We also didn't need to spend a lot of money on uniforms for school. We wore our blue and white uniforms every day. Oftentimes we even wore them as pyjamas to bed and if we needed to attend a more formal function, our school uniform looked respectable enough to wear to those events as well.

Our family did not have enough money to buy me more than one outfit. I had my school uniform and one very practical dress, or *shalwar kameez*, that had a simple sash that draped across the chest that I could wear every day.

There were small issues with having the classrooms inside the church. For instance, there wasn't always a lot of natural light inside the church. When the electricity was not working and candles were too expensive, it was not easy to read and write.

In all there were only thirty-five students attending St. Philip's Primary School, so it was easy to know everyone by name. The school's goal was to educate children well enough so they could compete for a spot in one of the local secondary schools. By the time I was only nine years old, I had already fallen behind the academic level of other students my age attending better schools. To get into secondary school, I would need to learn how to read and write. I had not achieved that yet.

I did not know it, but that day would be my final day of school.

3

GROWING UP QUICKLY

"Go, Shagufta! It's your turn!" the other girls shouted. I held the stick in my hand, tossed it in front of me, and watched as it bounced into one of the boxes etched in the dirt, directly in front of my feet. The stick landed in the third box to the left. Concentrating on both my rhythm and balance, I jumped into the first box with one foot. Then I hopped into the second and fourth box with one foot and landed in the final two boxes with two feet solidly planted into two boxes at the end. By thrusting my hips, I jumped in the air with a 180-degree turn and landed with both my feet in the respective boxes.

We were playing *shatapu*. Shatapu is a game very similar to hopscotch and was my favorite game during recess time in the church yard. I had my eyes focused on the stick in the third box. I had to retrieve it while maintaining my balance and keeping my feet in the proper box.

In fairness, it was easier to play shatapu as a Christian, because I didn't have to wear the extra clothing that Muslim girls were forced to wear. Our school didn't have many requirements imposed on students, but most schools in Pakistan required girls to be conservatively dressed with their hair covered. Most Pakistanis could tell that I was not a Muslim simply by looking at me. I didn't cover myself in the traditional garments that would be common for a young Muslim girl.

When I finished my round of shatapu, I tossed the stick on the ground, waved good-bye to my friends, and quickly ran home to my parents who were waiting for me to help prepare dinner.

The mood was strangely somber when I arrived home. My father was home and had been sick all day. He was not able to work. Missing one day of work was a big financial loss for our family of nine members. We needed income every day. The number of days my father missed work directly correlated to the number of days that we would have to miss eating. It was a simple formula. If my father did not work, we did not eat.

Both of my parents were hard workers; they were determined and willing to take any job they could find to feed us. At one point they had a small shop where they sold grain as animal food. They would work in the fields in the early morning hours to gather grain and then rush to the market to sell it. During cotton season, they would do the same thing.

They also worked as vegetable farmers. There was a wealthy farmer who grew different types of vegetables in his field. He would allow my parents to cultivate a certain portion of his land and he would pay them in vegetables for the work they did.

"Hello, Shagufta," said an older rotund man from our village, stroking his beard as he approached me. "Is your father home? My wife needs a ride into town."

I shook my head as I gave him a morose glance, sad that I would disappoint him. "I'm sorry, ummm…" I struggled to remember his name. I had it on the tip of my tongue, but it would not come to me, "but he is not feeling well."

"Ok then," he replied without as much disappointment as I thought he would have. "I'll ask again tomorrow. I hope he gets well soon."

I waved at him, and he turned and left. His departure marked yet another job that my father often did to bring money into the family. We didn't have a car, but we were one of the few families that had a horse and *tanga*, or cart, that taxied people from village to village. Our horse and cart could carry seven people and their belongings like a metro mini-bus. We were the village "Uber" that people called when they needed a ride.

With my father sick and my mother tending to him, I started working on dinner. I poured oil from the square metal tin and watched small beads of oil cackle in the hot black pan. My mother observed from under the tarp that provided shade on the side of our house.

Our house was too warm to be inside. The brick house acted like a tandoori oven with the sun directly overhead, and my father found a pleasant breeze that cooled him while laying outside in the *charpai khaat*. The charpai is an elevated cot that we use to sleep on to keep us off the ground. The English word "cot" is borrowed from khaat with four (*char*) legs (*pai*).

My mother stroked his head. He was clearly growing weaker.

All of our charpai khaats were scattered outside. It was simply too warm in the evenings to sleep inside.

"Asaf?" I shouted, not seeing him, but knowing he was somewhere behind me. "Can you fetch me some water?"

Silence was my only response. "Asaf!" I demanded louder, but he still didn't answer.

"Nasarin?" I shouted, changing my tactic, knowing that it would be more of a fight to get Joseph or Asaf to do it. "Please bring me some water."

"Okay," came the easy response. Without hesitation, she picked up a large cream-colored basin and walked over to the water pump in the middle of our courtyard, pushed through the goats, swatting them away with her hand, and began pumping the water. The goats were attempting to push their way over to the shade of the tarp to escape the direct heat of the sun, but I used my spatula to rustle them toward the shade tree instead.

With the oil simmering hot, I began to fry the flatbread while also chopping the potatoes and vegetables that we had left. I rationed out what we had so that everyone would get a small portion. For the third night in a row, we would not have meat.

Meat was too expensive, so we only had it once or twice a week. When we did eat meat, it was usually chicken and we would have to eat it the same day, because we didn't have a refrigerator to keep it in. Beef was a rare delicacy reserved for holidays and weddings.

"What are you cooking?" Rachel asked in her tiny voice. She was standing in her bare feet, gripping the dusty ground with her toes as she talked.

"I am making dinner, and if you can help look after your little brother Gasha, perhaps we can make some *marunda* together."

Rachel's face immediately lit up. "Yay!" she shouted, putting her hands together in a prayer grip and excitedly jumping up and down. The sweetened puffed rice treats were her favorite. They were simple and cheap to make, using only rice, milk, and sugar and were often successful in lifting grim moods.

"Can we watch television after dinner?" Nasarin asked, coming back with the heavy basin of water. She walked with her back arched slightly backward, trying to balance the basin with her weight to compensate for her small size.

"I don't know," I teased. "I don't know if there is anything worth watching tonight," knowing that tonight was our family's favorite family night to watch television.

"There is!" shouted Nasarin, shocked that I had forgotten. "*Ainak Wala Jin* is on tonight!"

"Are you sure?" I teased again, making Nasarin throw her hands up in the air in exasperation. "I know, I know!" I retorted when I saw that Joseph and Rachel were about to jump in if I didn't relent.

Ainak Wala Jin was our favorite comedy drama from Lahore about a genie who lives with a boy and his father and their magical adventures. Our family had the only television in the entire village. No family in our village was wealthy enough to buy one, but several aunts and uncles joined together and contributed to buy one together, so when we watched television, it was never alone, but with anyone in the village who wanted to join.

Getting the television ready to watch a program was almost as adventurous as watching it. The electricity was never stable, and we never knew when we would have electricity and when we would not.

The signal reception from Lahore was never perfectly aligned, so my father and uncles would have to play with the antenna, attaching it to the roof of our house and moving it around until it was perfect. It was always a volley of banter going from one uncle on the roof to another on the ground watching the black and white screen and waiting for the picture to come in as perfect as possible.

"What about now?" came the question from the roof, as my uncle or father would aimlessly point the antenna in the general direction where they thought there would be decent reception.

"No....no...." we would all say in unison waiting for something visible to come from the black and white snowy screen. "Now!" we all shouted as something that looked like a face or a car that we recognized appeared. Then, just as fast as it appeared, it would be gone again. "Nope! Go back! Go back!" we again all shouted. This often went on for long periods of time with my father and uncles getting frustrated, while the rest of us found it comically entertaining.

As soon as Rachel heard that we were having marunda and watching a comedy drama on television, she went and told our cousins. In our village, we were never in want of friends. Several of my parents' siblings bought village houses together so that we could all be close. We always had the comfort of having family friends close by.

Sometimes our cousins were closer to us than many knew. Deep in our village hid a special secret, and it went to the depths of our family's close-knit ties.

My uncle and his wife were never able to have a child of their own. They had tried and tried, but it was not medically possible. The doctor told them that they would never have children together.

My mother and father were not wealthy, but they were blessed more than most when it came to the ease of which they had children. So, my mother gifted my uncle with one of her children.

Between my two youngest siblings, my mother had a baby that few knew about. She never publicly announced her pregnancy. After my mother gave birth to a baby girl, she presented her newborn daughter to her brother as a gift to him and his wife. They were so excited and never had there been a child doted on more than her.

After dinner, I cleaned up, watching my mother's worried face as she applied a cool cloth to my father's head. I set up a barrier of cots to keep the animals from walking into the kitchen space as I washed up the bowls, pans, and utensils. I have seen my father ill before, but there was something different about this time. There was a look of concern on my mother's face.

I slowly dried one of the bowls and strained my ear to hear them talking. I desperately wanted to know what was causing them so much concern. I slowed my breathing to listen to their conversation. I could hear mumblings of their discussion, but someone was banging the wood around the squatting trench that we used as our toilet at the back corner of the yard. The smell of the small rivulet that flowed out from underneath the outhouse into a stream of the village's raw sewage made a slight trickling sound.

Finally, after drying the last dish, I stood up, straightened out my legs and walked over to where they were. My father tried to turn his head to look at me, but he was simply too weak to make eye contact.

"Is everything okay, Mother?" I asked.

She answered by simply shaking her head no. She was silent for a short moment and then, while still looking at him, she said, "It's tuberculosis."

I had never heard the word before and didn't know what it meant. It sounded nefarious and malicious, like the name of a ghost that floats in the air and suddenly attacks people at will.

I stood in shocked silence, not making a sound. It seemed that she had not told anyone else, and I was the first to know. I stood waiting for her to tell me that he was going to die. From the look on her face, I was convinced that death was the only outcome.

"He will be okay, Shagufta," she said, almost understanding that I was expecting the worst, "but we all are going to need to pull together to survive."

She didn't say it. She didn't have to. She and the family needed me to find a job to make money. Her silence communicated the damning news that I would need to drop out of school and look for work to support them.

4

SUPPORTING THE FAMILY THROUGH HARDSHIP

"Shagufta, you must be careful around the Muslims. You are guilty no matter what you do," my mother said, trying to warn me before I left out for my first job. I listened intently to her words. It was easy to forget how dangerous it was for Christians in Pakistan because the Muslims in our village were kind and loving. I even played with them sometimes.

"I am sorry that you don't know these things, Shagufta. Your father and I wanted to protect you. It's why we live here, close by Christian family members. It's why we live in this village that has its own church. It's why we sent you to a Christian school. We wanted to keep you and your brothers and sisters safe, but out there," she said, pointing away from the house and then lowering her voice as if someone was secretly listening, "out there are people who do not believe anyone should have faith in a religion different than theirs. There are Muslims who do not see you as human, and they hate you."

"But why?" I asked, a bit confused. "How can they hate me? They don't know me."

"They know you are a Christian, and that is enough. In their teachings, Christians are unclean."

"Unclean?" I said looking at my skin and clothes. "But I just bathed, and my clothes were washed two days ago."

"It doesn't matter," my mother replied. "You can bathe a thousand times and wear brand-new clothes and still be dirty in their eyes. Listen to me, Shagufta. You will always be unclean, and that means that you will always be wrong. You will always be guilty—even for things that you did not do."

The idea of being guilty of things that I did not do seemed impossible. Surely people could not be that blatantly hateful. Maybe they were biased against Christians, but to just pin crimes on innocent Christians? I was not completely convinced.

My mother undoubtedly saw the disbelief spelled out on my face, because she followed up with a simple, "It is better to keep your head down and keep quiet. Do your job and do not cause any trouble."

I felt the emotion that my mother poured out to me that morning. Everything was new and scary. I slowly turned to leave, but mother pulled on my arm, hoping to warn me further.

"Do not argue with anyone, and if you are blamed for anything, do not even try to defend yourself. Avert your eyes, look down at the ground, and walk away. Trust me when I say that you will never win an argument. As Christians, we must shut our mouths and silence ourselves."

"Even if I am blamed for something I didn't do?" I protested.

"Christians are blamed for everything, Shagufta. If Muslims injure themselves kicking you, you will be blamed for bruising their foot. If you are accused of anything, you must not say anything. Leave it to God. God will be your salvation in your time of need. He will be your protector."

I bowed my head and felt helpless. I didn't want to cause trouble. I didn't want to cross paths with Muslims and anger them for no reason. I just wanted to work and make money for my family so we could eat.

"Our country is changing," she said. I could see that she was struggling to put her thoughts into words that I would understand, but I understood much more than she knew. Our family were poor farmers and did not understand much about politics, but no one could escape the drama.

Our former leader had been overthrown by the military and was imprisoned and hanged in our state province of Punjab. We couldn't turn on the television to watch our most beloved programs without hearing the news of the dramatic shifts. Overnight, the new president of Pakistan made "Shariazation" the centerpiece of his new government.

It seemed there were sweeping Islamic revivals taking place every time we turned the television on. The nation of Iran had just seen an Islamic revolution a few years earlier where the president was overthrown in a military coup, like in our country. I didn't even know where Iran was.

News personalities in Pakistan were cheering for the Islamic leaders. Our new president wanted to make Pakistan pure in their adherence to Islam, like the new government in Iran was doing. The word *Pakistan* means "land of the pure," and he wanted to make it pure again.

My parents, aunts, uncles, and neighbors gathered around the television most nights, not to watch comedy dramas, but to see an update on the daily news. They watched with much interest as the new Islamic governments took over in Pakistan. I didn't understand all the rapid changes at the time, but it was clear that they were worried that the new Pakistan was going to be less tolerant to Christian minorities like us.

"This is not good," my uncle said one night after the announcement that the former Prime Minister had been executed. My father didn't respond. He just shook his head and looked at the ground.

"There is no one to stop General Muhammad Zia-ul-Haq."

"Not here!" my father said, quickly interrupting him with a grunt and a hand wave. "Not now in front of the children."

"What? They can't see? Their world is changing in front of our eyes. It's not a secret. Sharia courts are replacing common judicial courts. New laws incorporating Islamic Sharia law have now been established. Now we have punishments for speaking against Islamic law such as whipping, amputations, stoning, and hanging? Where does it stop?"

My father's eyes bulged at my uncle, commanding him to stop speaking without saying a word. With a growl, trying to disguise itself as a whisper, he said, "If you are heard saying that do you understand what would happen? Worse yet, what if the children repeat what you are saying to the wrong person? Do you understand what could happen to them?"

There was a moment of silence before my uncle just shook his head and walked away.

Without saying it directly, my mother was acknowledging the fear my uncle had expressed that night. Our reality as Christians in Pakistan had changed, and the danger was ever present.

"You have to be a silent lamb," she said, stroking her hand over my head. "I am sending you out like sheep among wolves...."

"What does that mean?" I asked her.

"Jesus said it to His disciples in the Bible," she said. "It means that you are being sent out into the world knowing that everyone is against you. A sheep doesn't have to do anything to be attacked by the wolves. It simply exists. The sheep has no power to defend itself from the wolf. It must rely completely on the Shepherd for protection. If you are hated, you must respond with love. If you are mistreated, you must respond with kindness. If you are accused, you must not retaliate in anger or hate. A sheep has no power on its own against the wolves. The Shepherd will provide. The Shepherd will be your protector, and He will be your salvation against the wolves."

"So, you are saying that I am being sent out like a sheep?"

"Yes, my darling daughter. You are being sent out like a silent lamb among the wolves."

It was not an easy thing for my nine-year-old mind to understand, but when I thought of the sheep in our village and how the owner of the sheep provided for them and protected them, then I understood more. I imagined the words of Jesus in the Bible, sending out sheep, like the ones in my village, and protecting them as they went.

After talking with my mother, I didn't want to leave to work in the fields. I wanted to stay in our village where it felt safer. I wanted to play hide-and-go-seek with my friends at school; one of my favorite games. I wanted to be with my family in the evening and watch my father and uncle mess with the antenna, attempting to get the perfect reception so that we could all carelessly laugh at the adventures of *Ainak Wala Jin* on our little black and white television, but I knew that I could not.

Our family had run out of food and money. We had to sell our animals to buy medicine for my father and did not have any money left. This was the only option.

5

ISLAM 101

"**S**hagufta? Are you Christian?" the landowner's wife asked with a disgusted snarl, as if saying the word would make her unclean.

"Yes, aunty," I replied. Shagufta is not a traditional Christian name, but it is different from the Muslim names in Punjab, and it made me stand out. I was marked. There was no escaping it in Pakistan. Not only did my name mark me, but I was marked as a Christian on my birth certificate and identification. Even passports were marked at that time and are a different color for Christians so that they are identified before even opening them.

Several girls standing around me silently shifted away when they heard that I was a Christian.

It happened very often that the employers would treat me differently as soon as they learned that I was Christian. They

45

would give me the lowest level jobs for the smallest amount of pay. I was okay with that. I had to be. I didn't have a choice if I wanted to earn money for our family.

The landowners in Punjab did not want to hire Christians to work in their fields, but they did not have enough Muslims willing to do the lowly hard labor jobs for low pay. Over time I learned the system. I was accustomed to the day-labor market and how to best get hired. I knew exactly where to stand in the marketplace to find the landowners that needed workers for their fields. Today I was selected to work in a potato field.

Plucking potatoes is hot, back-breaking work, but it was a job that was often given to women. It was simple, but not easy. My job was to follow behind a tractor that ploughed over potato mounds. A large mechanism on the back of the tractor churned through the soil, pulling the potatoes to the surface. I walked behind and gathered the potatoes in piles, then carried them to a collection point.

Plucking potatoes was not much different than my first job of picking cotton.

Unlike potatoes, picking cotton is not paid a set price by the hour. Instead, I was paid by the kilogram. To make enough money to make it worthwhile, I had to run up and down the rows, picking as much cotton as I could in the shortest amount of time possible.

I was given my own row of cotton plants and a bag to collect the cotton in called a *choele*. My tan bag with flannel brown stripes was almost as big as I was. The wide linen straps of the bag fit perfectly on my forehead and put the weight directly on my head and neck, which allowed me to carry more weight. The bag hung down behind my back but could swing to my side for easy access as I picked the cotton. When the bag got heavier, I used two additional straps at the side of the bag to tie around my waist. This helped spread the load from my waist to my hips. When the bag was full, it was heavier than me!

The cotton plants were in some ways easier than the potatoes because the cotton plants were about three to four feet high and didn't require as much crouching down and bending over as potatoes did.

The challenge with picking cotton is that the plant surrounding the white fluffy "fruit" is a rough thorny crown that has a way of pricking your fingers every time you go in to pull out the cotton. I learned to put my fingers into a small clamp to move into the plant, but it was not always successful. The thorns ripped my hands and fingers open day after day. I had blood on my hands, on my clothes, on my bag and even on the cotton that I was picking.

I hustled from one plant to the next so that I could attempt to make more money, but the aunty in the field watching me would scream if she saw me skip over lower, smaller blooms of cotton. It was much faster to move down the plants and grab the biggest clumps of cotton. Those would quickly fill up my sack, but that technique also left a lot on the plant.

"Stop! Go back!" she would holler if she saw me skip anything.

My first boss was a short round woman who diligently covered her head and neck with a scarf. Her hardened leathery face, browned by constant exposure to the sun, always looked as if she had something sour in her mouth. Her scratchy voice had a base that found its stability in the drum of her rotund belly. She was a conservative Muslim and hated my existence. To her, I was a dog working in the field.

"Why does she hate me so much?" I asked one of ladies working beside me in the cotton field on the neighboring row one day. Talking to the other ladies always made the time go faster.

"Because you are Christian," she said, keeping her head down and continuing to pick cotton.

"But why though? Why does she hate Christians so much?"

"You don't know? Did you go to school at all?"

"Yes, I went to school," I said, defending myself.

"Were you not taught about the Qur'an?" she asked, perplexed that I had gone to school and not learned from the Qur'an. In Pakistan, every student must learn to recite the Qur'an.

"No, I went to a Christian school. We did not learn anything about the Qur'an."

"Oh, now I understand," she replied with sympathy in her voice. "Well, aunty went to a regular school and learned what we all know about Christians."

"And what is that?" I asked, suddenly feeling afraid to hear the answer.

"All schools teach that Christians are not patriotic, because they do not believe in the religion that our country is built upon."

"What?" I said in shock, stopping my stride and looking straight at her in disbelief. My family could have chosen to live in India, but they chose to live in Pakistan. "Well, that is not true. I am just a Pakistani as the next person and proud to be so."

"It's in our textbooks. Are you saying that you know more than our school textbooks?"

Suddenly, the words of my mother came back to me. "Silent lamb," I said to myself. "Be a silent lamb. This is your first job. Don't get in trouble."

"Our textbooks also say that Christians are unclean—like a pig or a dog," she said nonchalantly.

I wanted to speak up and say something, but how could I argue with a textbook? What experience did I have to argue with what she was saying? I had not even been to school long enough to learn how to read and write.

"And it is not just our textbooks," she continued. "It also says in the Qur'an that Christians are the enemy."

I froze. I didn't know that the Qur'an mentioned Christians. I thought it was a holy book for Muslims. Our Bible didn't say anything about Muslims, so I assumed that the Qur'an didn't say anything about Christians.

"Does the Qur'an mention Christians anywhere else?" I asked, careful not to cause offence with my question.

"Of course it does!" she said almost laughingly as if it was the dumbest question she had ever heard someone ask. "The Qur'an says that the followers of Jesus rejected the teaching of the Prophet, even when he was kind to them."

"So, the Prophet was peaceful to the Christians then," I said, immediately seizing on her own words. They were the words I had heard so many people say when explaining away the common violence we saw against Christians.

"Pfft...the Prophet extended nothing but peace to the Christians in the beginning, but they would not accept the truth. They rejected his teaching and abandoned him when he was kicked out of Mecca. That is why he gathered up his faithful followers and with his holy sword, he declared war against them. In the Holy Qur'an, he still commands us to follow his example and war against the unbelievers. The Holy Qur'an says, 'Those who follow Muhammad are merciless to unbelievers but kind to each other' (see Qur'an: Sūrah al-Fath 48:29). It also commands Muslims to make war on the unbelievers (see Qur'an: Sūrah at-Tawbah 48:29)."

"But can't Christians and Muslims be friends?" I almost whispered, hoping to end the conversation as quickly as possible before anyone heard. I regretted ever engaging in the conversation. The mere idea of me disagreeing with a Muslim could get me into trouble.

"Friends?" she repeated, as if I had missed something obvious. "The holy Qur'an tells Muslims not to take the Jews or the Christians as friends. They are only friends and protectors of each other, and Allah will turn on them that befriends them."

I gulped so loud that I was certain that she could hear it. In that moment, standing between rows of cotton, I realized how important it is to know what Muslims believe. Their source of hatred toward me did not come from their nature. We were all born in the same place, ate the same food, enjoyed the same weather, and spoke the same language, but the lens in which we saw the world was completely different.

"Our textbooks teach the history of how Christians from England oppressed the Muslims from Pakistan. Christians are on the side of the oppressors. Muhammad warned us how the Christians would treat us hundreds of years before England was even a country. He was right. The holy Qur'an is always true."

I had so much to say in response to her but couldn't utter a word. I had never been to England or met anyone from outside of Pakistan. Jesus was not from England; He was from the Middle East. He was not an oppressor who picked up a sword and killed unbelievers—He gave His life as a loving sacrifice for unbelievers. Muhammad taught his followers to kill those that did not accept Islam, but Jesus taught His followers to love our enemies as we love ourselves.

I could feel the words pushing past my teeth and bubbling my lips. I dearly wanted to say that Christians are not the enemy of Pakistan, but the friends of everyone. The pressure was building up, and I could almost feel it release against my will, but I did emerge triumphant and suppressed the thoughts away from my mouth, down my throat, and deep down into the pits of my stomach.

"I am sorry. I don't know so much about the Qur'an," I said, hoping that she would be gentle with me in my ignorance.

She didn't look up at me or acknowledge that I had even spoken to her. I was happy about it. I desperately wanted to be ignored. I wanted to be more insignificant than a pebble in her sandals.

Now as I picked potatoes, I remembered that conversation in the cotton fields. I had learned so much about picking cotton, Islam, and keeping quiet. That was the beginning of my education to help me understand why the aunty hated me so much.

It wasn't her fault that she hated me so much. She was taught as a child that Christians were enemies of Pakistan. They believed Christians were not patriotic enough to support the Islamic State of Pakistan. Not only were Christians enemies of Pakistan, but they were enemies of the Qur'an.

Without prompting, my cotton-picking companion had shared one last thought to ensure that my question was answered in full. "The Qur'an says that Muhammad is the Messenger of Allah and those who are with him are hard against the disbelievers, but tender among themselves."

We never spoke again during the rest of the picking season. I didn't want to risk being involved in that conversation again. I never told my mother about the incident, because I knew that she already worried too often about me.

At the end of that day, I collected my pay. I had earned about thirty Pakistani rupees that day, which is about ten cents in America. It was not much, but I was thankful to God for allowing me to work.

6

GOD'S LESSONS AMID PERSECUTION

"Don't touch anyone," I chanted to myself walking through the market. I kept my eyes on the ground and watched my feet navigate through the fine dust. I just needed to make it to the shop and purchase salt without anyone noticing me. The entire country was on edge, and Christians were being targeted.

A fourteen-year-old Christian boy named Salamat Masih had been sentenced to death for writing graffiti against the Prophet Muhammad, which had enraged Muslims all over the country. Suddenly it was as if every Christian in Pakistan were guilty of writing graffiti against the Prophet. Riots were breaking out in various cities, and mobs were demanding death by hanging. Salamat Masih had no education and was illiterate, but in Pakistan, all that needed to happen was the accusation.

Another Christian named Ayub Masih was making head-lines at the same time. He was a simple brick layer in a nearby Punjabi village and was arrested for allegedly sharing a book that Muslims hate called *The Satanic Verses*. The book was authored by Salman Rushdie, a former Muslim born in India. Many within the Muslim world wanted him hanged for writing the book. Ayub's entire village had to leave their homes and abandon their village because of the death threats issued toward them. Families and children that were not guilty of any crime other than sharing the same village as Ayub had to roam from village to village seeking safety from the angry mobs.

There didn't seem to be any rational reason for the violence against Christians. My father said the new Islamic laws of Pakistan were making everyone afraid of their neighbors and their fear appealed to man's lowest basic instinct. "They don't necessarily hate Christians," he said from his bed after watching the news. "They fear Islam."

Fear is a basic instinct that instinctively manifests itself into hate. Anyone with a phobia can easily identify with that premise. I have a strong sense of arachnophobia, or an extreme fear of spiders, and so I naturally hate spiders.

The daily propaganda against Christians created fear and evoked strong emotions of hate and anger. The violence and persecution that were playing out all over Pakistan were not emotion but were the effects of an emotional response.

My state province of Punjab was a powder keg about to explode because of the propaganda against Christians being pumped into the schools, newspapers, and mosques. It is not enough that Christians do not evangelize, and it is not enough

that they abide by Islamic law, but they are not able to even dis-
agree because so often disagreement can be called blasphemy.

A neighboring village about fifteen miles away from our
home was called Shanti Nagar. My mother's family was living
there when they were attacked by thirty thousand angry
Muslims. Their home was destroyed, and they ran to escape the
violence and barely survived. They were not alone. Hundreds of
homes were burned to the ground, thirteen churches destroyed,
and fifteen thousand Christians also had to run for their lives.[]
The anger of the mobs was ignited because someone said that
there was a Christian in the village who had ripped up the pages
of the Qur'an.

My uncles loaded a wagon full of food, blankets, and other
supplies and took it to Shanti Nagar to help the villagers,
including our family, survive. After all the damage and violence,
it turned out that the report about the desecration of the Qur'an
was not true!

I just wanted to buy one simple item for cooking and make
it back home before anyone saw me. We had just harvested the
year's wheat, and I needed to return home to cook. The violence
against Christians was in everyone's mind, and I simply wanted
to keep as low of a profile as possible.

My family and I had been cutting wheat for a family near
our village and trying to forget the violence in the rest of the
country. My mother, brothers, and sisters were all there to
assist. The harvest was one of the most important of the year
because we were paid for our labor, not in rupees, but in wheat.

The landowner needed to quickly harvest his wheat and
could not do it alone with his small staff, so he allowed our family

to work in his field and help process the grain, and in return he gave us a small corner of land to harvest our own wheat.

The allotment that he gave was enough for our family to use for the entire year. We were paid to cut the wheat according to how much wheat we cut. The more wheat we cut, the more wheat we earned. It was a simple barter of labor for goods between us and the landowner.

Although many farmers use tractors and combines to harvest their wheat, poor farmers in Punjab still use the same method as our ancestors. Our entire family had to be up and out of bed by four in the morning to get to the fields before the heat did. We worked all day in the heat of the sun, which often reached temperatures exceeding 110 degrees Fahrenheit, without breaking except for lunch and dinner. We had little time to rest or take a pause. If we didn't harvest it quickly enough, the unharvested wheat would all go bad and be wasted.

Every day we spent the morning cutting the wheat by grabbing a fistful of wheat and very carefully cutting it without cutting ourselves. After cutting the wheat, I laid it behind me and in the afternoon my young siblings would come, collect it, and tie it up in sheaves. After completing an entire row, the wheat was carried to a location where it would be thrashed to separate the grain from the chaff.

The entire process reminded me of a message I heard in church one time when John the Baptist told his followers that Jesus would baptize with the Holy Spirit and fire and will clear His threshing floor, gathering the wheat into His barn and burning up the chaff with an unquenchable fire. (See Matthew 3:11–12.)

There were so many parables that Jesus taught that made more sense to me after working on various farms.

One of my favorite parts of the Bible is when Jesus said that He is the Bread of Life that comes down from heaven, which we can eat and not die. (See John 6:35.) We eat flatbread at every meal. Our family could not live without it, just like we cannot live without the Bread of Life. The wheat that we had harvested was bread that we needed to sustain our lives on earth just like we needed His bread to sustain our spiritual lives for eternity.

As I took the new flour and made the *chapati,* I was again reminded of the Bible. Like the church, a good chapati needs four main ingredients.

First, you need the wheat that is separated from the chaff. Chaff grows together with the wheat, just as Christians live in the world with unbelievers, but when the day of harvest comes, the wheat is separated because chaff mixed with wheat makes it inedible. Wheat can bring nutrition to the body, but chaff brings illness, because chaff cannot be digested.

Second, salt is needed. Christ has called us to be the salt of the earth. If salt loses its saltiness, then it has no use (see Matthew 5:13), not even in chapati.

Third, water is added. Jesus said that He is the Living Water and whoever drinks of Him will never be thirsty again. (See John 4:14.) Water binds the salt and the wheat flour together when making chapati.

Fourth, there's oil. The oil is the anointing. In the chapati, oil allows higher cooking temperatures than water, aiding the food to cook faster and making it more flavorful. The anointing makes it possible for the church to endure persecution and brings flavor through the fires.

The chapatis I make have one more ingredient—animal excrement. It is hard to believe, but animal dung is an important part of cooking in the Punjabi region of Pakistan.

Our village is in a dry, arid region of Pakistan. Almost three quarters of Pakistan is dry and arid. In fact, Pakistan has the only existing fertile desert in the world. Like Pakistan, the church must learn to be fertile and reproduce even when the environment is like a spiritual desert.

Without natural forests, it is not possible to cook with wood, so we use the dung from our animals to make fires. Our brick home, like every home in our village, is decorated with large round mounds of animal dung that has been collected from our domestic farm animals, mixed with small shrubs and twigs, and then slapped on the side of our home to dry in the sun.

I used the dried dung for fuel and even though it is not necessarily added to the food, it is essential. The fire of the excrement is necessary to take all those ingredients and make bread.

The church in Pakistan needs go through all the dung that the world throws at us and be set in the fires of tribulation and persecution to consolidate all the elements that make us a church that gives the Bread of Life to the world.

Not long after that day that I successfully returned with the salt, we were hit by the excruciating news that our mother almost died because of our furnace.

Our *Mitti Ka Chulha*, or clay oven, is a handmade furnace. We use it every day to bake flatbread, and it needed repair. To repair it, we would go to the mountain where the clay is dug out.

While digging the clay by hand, deep in the cave, the entire cavern collapsed without warning. My mother was completely buried in the rubble with no oxygen and no feasible way to get out. I immediately began praying to the Lord as a team of villagers started digging for her. After a short period of time, the rescue team were able to dig my mother out, but her limp body showed no signs of life.

After praying for her, she started to breathe again, color returned to her cheeks, and she was saved!

It was a miracle that pointed to the reason why my simple faith in God never wavered.

7

MARRIAGE, FAMILY, AND A LIFE-ALTERING INCIDENT

I married Shafqat in the year 2000, after my uncle met a man looking for a bride for his son. "I know a good girl for him," my uncle said to him.

After the initial proposal by my uncle, Shafqat's family visited our home, and my family went and visited his home. They agreed on a bride price and the marriage was set.

The wedding was simple but special. Shafqat was a very attractive man on our wedding day. He was slim and taller than me with a strong, angular jawline that I found attractive. He had a friendly face and a meek disposition that shied away when our eyes first met.

He had a good job working in the city at a camera shop. Unlike my family who were all farmers, he had an office job making photos for passports, visas, and documents. His income was around one thousand five hundred rupees or six dollars per month, which was a good deal more than I could make in the fields, but it was not long after our wedding that he lost his job.

His boss was Muslim, as almost every employer is in Pakistan, and hired Shafqat for a fraction of the price of what other Muslim employees would make for the same job. It is hard for Christians to be hired for office jobs because those jobs are often reserved for Muslims.

In the cities, Christians minorities like Shafqat are mostly relegated to low-skilled jobs like sweeping streets, cleaning toilets, and collecting garbage. This is why Christians are often referred to as *Chura*. Chura is a derogatory term that originates from the name of a lower caste that is considered unclean. Chura do the dirtiest jobs in Pakistan. In Punjab, some of the earliest Christians came from a Chura, a lower caste of people that had darker skin. Even today, many of the Christians can be identified because of their darker skin. If a Christian is known to work at a business, other Muslims will not use that business because everything the Chura touches is unclean.

If Christians try to start their own business, they will find it almost impossible to get bank loans, find landowners to rent them business space, or maintain local supply chains for goods they need for their business.

If Christians are blessed enough to make it past all those hurdles and somehow find a way to grow a thriving business, it is only a matter of time before they are accused of some religious crime that forces them to hand over their business to a local Muslim.

It is not uncommon for Muslims to run up a bill at a Christian business and instead of paying it, they just accuse the Christian of saying something against the Prophet Muhammad and then walk away without paying.

A Punjabi Christian named Ashfaq Masih fell victim to this common practice. Ashfaq worked at a bicycle shop when Muhammad Irfan came in asking for extensive repairs to his bike. When Muhammad was asked to pay the bill for the repair work, Muhammad deviously asked Ashfaq not to charge him because he was a devout Muslim. Muhammad knew that he had Ashfaq trapped.

If Ashfaq agreed and let Muhammad leave, then Muhammad would not have to pay. If Ashfaq did not agree, then he would be insulting Islam. Ashfaq would be charged for blasphemy, and Muhammad would still not have to pay.

Ashfaq sadly shook his head and softly replied, "I can't give you the work for free."

"Why?" Muhammad pushed. "I am a devout Muslim. Don't you care? Are you a Muslim?

"No. I am not a Muslim. I follow Jesus."

That was all Muhammad needed. He barged out of the shop, filed a complaint, and within hours, Ashfaq was arrested and taken to jail and subsequently found guilty of blasphemy.

Shafqat's situation was infuriating but expected. His employer wanted to exploit him for the cheapest salary that he could get away with. He knew that Shafqat would not be able to find another job with any other business in the city and took advantage of him. He increased Shafqat's hours and workload while at the same time decreasing his pay.

When he finally lost his job, we were forced to leave our home and move to the city of Sahiwal to look for work. I had to be more vigilant in Sahiwal than in my hometown. Islamic customs were much stronger in Sahiwal than I was used to.

"Excuse me," I said as a reflex when I felt a hard bump into my back. I was not far from the cattle market, and the crowds were increasing to buy last minute items before the Friday holiday for Islamic prayer. I turned to see a frightened lady keeping her head down and moving quickly to avoid being noticed. I paused to see if she was alright.

She glanced up for only a moment and my breath stopped. Staring back at me was not the face of a woman, but of a monster. Partially hidden under a wide headscarf, patterned with dark earth tones that partially blocked the light, was a face that had melted off. Two dark eyes peeked out, unable to be hidden by eyelids, which were missing. Two black cavities in the shape of small opposing paisleys dented the center of her face where her nose should have been. Skin twisted and stretched like grey taffy across her face, reminding me of flowing lava running across the ground at the base of a volcano.

My heart stopped.

In that moment, all the stories that I had heard about women attacked with acid were verified. I had heard about them but had never come face-to-face with them.

Acid attacks on women are common in Pakistan. The most common reasons for attacks on women and girls are romantic rejection, such as the refusal of marriage or denial of sex. Some girls in Punjab have even been attacked with acid for simply looking at boys. The attacks are an expression of control over a woman's body. It is a statement of, "If I can't have you, no one can."

Acid attacks are one of the most diabolical forms of brutality against women because it kills a woman while she is still alive. Her face and sometimes body are disfigured in the ghastliest ways, sentencing her to a life of social rejection and disgust. Victims can't even look at themselves in the mirror, repulsed by disfigurement that has stolen their beauty.

In Pakistan, women are often considered mere extensions of men, without an identity of their own. Though Shafqat faced opposition because he was Christian, my status in the world was much lower. Not only was I a Christian, but I was also a woman. This put me at the lowest end of the social scale in Pakistan with virtually no worth.

In Sahiwal, certain laws known as the Hudood Ordinances were much more adhered to than in my small home village. The Hudood Ordinances enforced Islamic law by using harsh punishments for violations of Sharia Law, including stoning women to death for having sex outside of marriage or enforcing amputations for stealing.

Everyone knew that the Hudood laws were easy to convict and hard to acquit. Women were never offered a fair trial. Accusations alone were enough to be convicted and sentenced to death.

Most of the time, women accused of sexual immorality never made it to trial. Women, both Christian and Muslim, have the burden of carrying their family's honor, and if they are accused of such a crime, they are often killed by their own family to save the family's honor.

In Sahiwal I had to remain vigilant and on alert, venturing out only when I could do so together with Shafqat. Christian women are often targets of kidnapping and rape. Rape victims without four or more witnesses of the rape are punished under the Hudud laws as adultery.

Reports of young Christian girls who had been followed, kidnapped, and raped by older Muslim men were on the rise. The women who were raped were either forced to marry their rapist or threatened with prison or death. It was a terrible situation.

I managed to stay close to Shafqat. I always felt safe around him. He is two years younger than me, but he had a level of street smarts that gave me comfort. No matter what was wrong, I was certain that he would find a way to fix it. The longer we were married, the more I loved him.

Not long after arriving in the city, we began working on our family. In 2001, I gave birth to Zain. He was the most beautiful, perfect baby boy that there ever was. My second child, Danish, was born two years later, and Sheroz, my third son, was born in 2005.

We didn't have much money, so I tried to save every penny by making my own blankets for the babies. I wasn't educated, but I understood children. I had been taking care of my siblings my entire life and had dreamed of having my own babies since I was a little girl. I dreamed about singing my baby to sleep while rocking it back and forth in my arms. In my spare time in between daydreaming, I collected raw cotton, spun it to yarn and made my own baby clothes.

Shafqat spent the days out in the market trying to find a job to support our new and growing family. It was not long before he found a job that would change the trajectory of our lives forever.

Shafqat's youth and energy made him extremely employable, but it was counterbalanced by his religion. He also had experience working in an office, which made him marketable in the city, but his faith also made him somewhat of a liability. He was determined to find a job, no matter what obstacles he had to overcome. His confidence and street intelligence led him to a connection with a debt collection group.

The group was hired to collect debts when debtors failed to pay their bills on time. Like all debt collectors, they used several different tactics to apply the maximum amount of pressure for people to pay the money they owed.

To collect money, companies use many different approaches in Pakistan. They begin by sending an excessive number of letters and phone calls. Their hope is that they can create pressure by reminding a client of their obligation over and over again.

If that does not work, then they increase the pressure by contacting family members and creating an environment of shame. Shaming someone is extremely effective in Pakistan. Honor and shame are powerful means of social control, especially in Punjabi culture.

If shaming a family does not work, then debt collecting agencies dramatize the situation, exaggerating the true nature of the debt, reach out to employers, and threaten wage garnishment.

Shafqat was on a security detail that made personal visits to people that owed money. Their presence was meant to intimidate and create an urgency to pay the bill, but one day while looking for a man that had not been paying his debt, the pressure was tipped to the point of retaliation. Shafqat went to the man's factory where the man worked to apply pressure, when the company's security team pulled out a gun and began shooting.

Shafqat was shot in the back. He fell to the ground and lay there in a pool of his own blood. The bullet smashed through his spine and left him paralyzed from the waist down.

8

EXPERIENCING GOD'S ANSWERED PRAYER

Much of life is struggling. There is a struggle between what we wish for life to be like and what unfolds as we live it. I didn't desire anything more than raising a simple family in a small village in Punjab where I grew up. I dreamt of watching my children running to church for early morning prayers just as I had, returning home for warm flatbread and chai and playing with a dog like my Jackey-Jackey.

What unfolded was different than I had anticipated. I never planned for Shafqat to be handicapped. I never dreamed of a world where he would never walk again. The man that I married would no longer be able to work as he once had. Just as I had done when my father was sick, I would have to return to work in the fields to help my family survive.

Not long after I returned to work, Shafqat and I gave birth to a baby girl and named her Sara. At that time Shafqat's aging father moved in with us and was an additional mouth to feed.

I looked for a job that would allow me to make money and care for my children at the same time, but there was not much available for a poor, uneducated, illiterate girl like me in the city of Sahiwal.

When I prayed the Lord's Prayer as Jesus taught His disciples (see Matthew 6:5–15), the words came alive for me. They had a powerful meaning now. When I uttered the words, "Lord, give us this day our daily bread," I knew that I was literally crying out to Him to give us bread for the day. It was no longer just a metaphor; it was my reality. Living in the moment was not a meditation practice that I adopted to obtain a Zen state of mind. My prayer time was not some simple spiritual appreciation for every moment that God had given to us. The Lord's Prayer was survival. I had no choice. I needed Him. I was living hand-to-mouth and needed my "daily bread." We didn't have enough food for the next day. I needed God's mercy more than ever as our family grew.

We had nowhere to live and nowhere to go.

I soon found a job taking care of livestock. A Muslim man with a small farm outside of the city center had cows, chickens, goats, and ten buffalo and needed help caring for them. Muslims often hire Christians to look after their animals because we are considered to be just as unclean as the animals are. Feeding them, cleaning them, shepherding them, and picking up their excrement are all considered worthy of our allotment in life.

In return for caring for the animals, I was given a small room to live in with my family. The room was not enough for our entire family to live in, but we were able to squeeze in under one roof and it kept us from being homeless on the streets.

My new boss saw the desperate situation that I was in and instead of helping us began demanding I do more work than I was capable of doing in a day. He was ready to take advantage of us and squeeze out every last bit of work from me that he could. I was basically working without pay, but he wanted more.

I was afraid to say no to any of his requests for fear that our family would be kicked out of the small room that he let us shelter in and left homeless. Our situation invited predators that wanted to prey on our situation.

"Where will you go if you leave here?" the booming Muslim man would say if I delayed answering his bellowing commands. "Do the work or you will be out on the streets. It's your choice." His threatening ultimatums came daily.

I prayed to the Lord day and night for reprieve. I found myself constantly thinking of Joseph in the Bible when he was a slave in Potipher's house and how Joseph's dreams and reality were so far apart when he was a slave (see Genesis 39–41). My dreams were not as grand as Joseph's dreams were, but still the chasm between my meager dreams and my reality was worlds apart.

After caring for the ten buffalo all day and providing them enough water for the evening, I made my way to the back corner of the boss's house where no one could see me. I slinked down into the fetal position, bringing my knees up to my chest and clutching the extra material that gathered around my ankles. My body shook uncontrollably.

"I can't continue on like this," I cried, hoping that God could hear me, even though I had no proof that He did. "I can't," I moaned again, wondering if God could understand when I prayed to Him in Urdu. I had nothing more to say and no more energy to say it. My stomach ached in pain and rumbled with hunger. I knew my children were feeling the same hunger pains, and I couldn't do anything to take those pains away.

My little Sara would soon be crying for me to give her milk. My body could barely produce enough moisture to cry—how would I have enough to feed her? I pulled my ankles closer to my thighs, pushed my head deeper into my knees, and begged for deliverance.

I remembered the priest in our village church teaching a message one time about "God never giving us more than we can handle."

"I am at my limit," I whispered quietly, hoping the Lord would hear me and release me from my trials. I prayed for Him to see that I could not handle any more. "I cannot continue, dear Lord. Please deliver us!" Those were the last words that I remembered repeating that evening before I fell asleep.

I woke up the next morning in my bed to the sound of someone saying my name. Looking down, I could see Sara sleeping in the crook of my arm. I was not certain how we got there. I was careful not to stir and wake her. An orphaned ray of light cut through the dusty air and showed on her face, bringing an angelic glow to her round chunky brown cheeks. Slowly and with one solid held breath as if I were about to dive under water, I pulled my right arm from under her head.

"Keep sleeping, my darling angel," I quietly whispered to her. The more she could sleep, the less she would think of food.

"Shagufta!" I heard again from outside in the courtyard.

I jolted up without disturbing too much of the room around me with the hopes of making it out the door and not waking anyone up.

When I walked out the door, I saw my uncle looking in the opposite direction and about to say my name again.

"Over here," I said in a yelled whisper. "Shh...uncle! Over here!" I waved my hands to grab his attention, as if he could see me from behind his head.

Immediately he turned and looked in my direction and began walking purposefully in my direction. I rubbed my eyes, trying to quickly adjust to the morning sun. I was a bit embarrassed that the sun had risen before I had. I hadn't even started my day and was already running late on my chores.

"Shagufta," my uncle said, his face brightening when I approached him. His square, narrow jaw, still visible through his beard, was the only difference that he had from my mother's appearance. His eyes, nose, and even the way he puckered his lips when he said my name were the same as hers.

"I am sorry, uncle; I didn't expect you to be here this morning. If my employer sees you here, I might get into trouble," I said, hoping he would state his purpose quickly and be on his way.

"After hearing my news, Shagufta, you might not need this job any longer," he replied with a mischievous smile that stretched from cheek to cheek.

I froze in place and stared at him. My arms hung limply down by my side as I leaned in to hear him tell me the news he had come to share. If there was anything that would better my situation, then I was eager to hear more.

"What?" I asked, not knowing what he meant.

"I found you a new job, Shagufta—and one much better than this one."

I clasped my hands together and brought them into my chest. I didn't know what the job was, but anything was better than what I had. "What is it!" I begged, not able to wait even a second longer for the news.

"I spoke to Bishop John Samuel, and he said that you could come with your family to work in the school." I had heard the bishop's name before but didn't know much about him. He ran a Christian school in the city of Gojra, about two hours from Sahiwal.

"Collect all your things and let's go talk to him. He is ready to hire you."

Without hesitating, I pivoted around and ran to the room, completely unaware of leaving my uncle standing in the middle of the courtyard.

We gathered everyone and everything and moved to the city of Gojra.

The city of Gojra is along the railway to the city of Faisalabad and did not look special in any way when we drove through, but the refuge that it offered promised more than any other place that I could think of.

When our van pulled up to the tan metal gates of the school compound, I could feel bubbling anxiety rising in my throat. I had not even been hired yet, but just the idea of working for Christians and with Christians was enough to excite me. Looking out the window I could see a large green sign with carefully painted white letters.

"What does the sign say?" I asked the driver as we pulled up.

Without looking at me, he shrugged and said, "It's in English, but I think it says, St. John's Cathedral High School. That is the name of the school, so I would assume that is what is painted there." Then squinting his eyes and peering below his visor, he continued, "I can read that small word on the end. It says Gojra."

The smaller word *Gojra* was hanging on the end as if the artist that painted the words ran out of room on the green sign and painted them small so that they would fit. Above the English words were also white Arabic font and I assumed that it said the same as the English.

To the left of the gate was a large plastic blue, yellow, and purple poster with faces of what I assumed to be local politicians running for local office. The poster had been weathered from weeks of sun and sand, but no one had bothered to remove it, though it had been heavily battered.

The school seemed like a palace to me, guarded by a full-time rotation of guards, ready to protect the inhabitants inside from outsiders who would wish them harm. There were two square concrete pillars on each side of the gate with an entrance to the right where the guards stood waiting for us to get out of our vehicle. In front of the gate were two black and yellow iron poles mounted in the ground with a thick black steel chain stretching between them to keep vehicles from passing before reaching the iron gate.

In front of the guard gate was a green plastic overhang providing protection for visitors from the sun and rain as they processed a security pass. I hugged Sara tightly as we got out of the van. It was a dream come true to think that I might be living on the other side of that security gate with my family. Security for our family, as Christian minorities, meant more than all the wealth in the world.

As we walked into the school, past the guard house, I looked down and noticed the patterned red brick under my feet. Instead of the typical ash and dirt that I walked on every day, the entire walkway was elevated with carefully laid brick that formed a pattern of squares that seemed to go on forever.

Well-trimmed square bushes lined the path and were only broken by perfectly manicured grass. I had never seen such green grass in my entire life. It was as if I were walking into a heavenly garden instead of a school. Behind the bushes and providing shade for the large patches of grass were tall, broad cedar trees.

In the middle of the brick-covered schoolyard was a tall blue and white statue in the shape of an umbrella with a small, elevated concrete platform where students could sit. Atop of the blue and white structure was the comfort of a large white cross. The cross looked like a symbol of refuge for me, after having crossed the desert lands of employment by thorny Muslim bosses.

Each of the tan buildings was filled with the echoing sounds of children laughing, shouting, and learning. My heart was so full that I felt that I would burst. I couldn't help but dream of my children attending such a school.

St. John's school hired me as a cleaner. In return for my work, the school would allow my children to attend for free, as well as let us live on the school compound in a corner unit.

Standing in the schoolyard, I found myself breaking free from the life that bound me to suffering and fear. I once again began dreaming of a simple family life like the one I had in a small village in Punjab growing up, but now reality was better than I had dreamed.

What unfolded was different than I had anticipated. I never planned for Shafqat to be handicapped, but without his situation my uncle would have never been able to secure a job for me at the school and my children would not have the opportunity that now lies before them.

My Father in heaven had indeed heard my prayers and provided my daily bread. I understood that He did speak Urdu after all!

9

EVACUATING THE SHEEP

"We have to leave tonight when it gets dark," Mary told me with a bereaved voice that seemed to beg me not to be afraid. Lulls cycled through our conversations, allowing us to listen to the silence, hoping to hear something, but we were glad when we didn't.

Mary was about thirty-five years old, with a bold-looking face, thick black hair, and brown freckles. A broad scarlet embroidered sash draped from her left shoulder and hugged her waist while she sat across from me. Her wide eyes glistened as she kept staring at the door as if it were to burst down at any time.

Mary came to comfort me, but she was the one that needed comfort. She attempted to calm her fear by bringing hope to us. Mary knew that Shafqat was in a wheelchair and not able to leave the compound in a hurry if the school was attacked.

"Tonight, we have a driver who will take you out of here. You will have to be very quiet, so that no one sees you leaving the compound." I nodded in agreement. We had a relative that we would go and stay with.

"What about the children?" I asked.

"The children are being sent to homes all around the city, to secretly stay with members of the church and friends of the school."

I nodded again, already knowing that most of the children had been evacuated. "Now we need to get your children out of the school," Mary said, looking around the room as if counting all four of them with her eyes. She looked down at the floor, ready to say something more, but took a deep breath instead. Her right leg bounced rapidly up and down. She looked up, but again nothing came out. She just sighed loudly and looked around the room.

"Why does Pakistan have to be like this?" Mary finally burst out. "Why are Christians so hated? What did we do for them to want to kill us like this?"

"It will be okay," I said, attempting to calm her down by speaking with slow, deliberately soft words. "Come now, would you like some tea?"

Mary nodded her head.

"Do you know the latest news?" I asked, hoping to hear that nothing more had happened.

"Eight Christians were burned alive!" she blurted out.

I gasped, putting my hands over my mouth.

"Eight Christians have been burned alive for doing nothing more than holding on to their faith! Their homes were attacked, burned to the ground, and their families are on the run. The entire city is up in flames, and we are next. Everyone knows that our school is a Christian school. The Muslims think we are to blame for the blasphemy."

"Eight Christians?" I asked, horrified. I hadn't heard the news. "Do you think they want to attack our school? Do you really think they would harm the children?"

She looked up with horror in her eyes. "Children? Children do not matter to them, Shagufta! They hate that this school teaches Jesus to children. They would rather the children be dead than to have them taught about Jesus. Two of the eight people that were burned alive last night were young teenage girls and one was only a seven-year-old child!" Mary sobbed with her face in her hand. "The police just stood by and allowed it to happen! They didn't even try to stop it. Not even our children are safe from their fits of anger."

I glanced over at Shafqat. We both knew that the high walls of the school would not keep the mobs out. Things had grown more dire than I had imagined. The city was falling, and Christians were prey.

The passions were ignited when a Christian had been accused of desecrating pages of the Qur'an at a wedding ceremony. The charges were not proven, but they didn't need to be proven. The accusation only needed to be hurled.

Many workers at the school speculated that the attacks were not the result of anything that happened with the Qur'an but were an excuse for Muslims to get their revenge on Christians because of the United States' war in Afghanistan.

"American dogs!" was the common name that people called us out on the streets when we left the school compound. Christians were less than one percent of the population in Punjab and posed no threat to anyone, so we were easy targets.

"American dogs" was not the only insult they hurled at us. Even Muslim children felt entitled to scream some of the vilest insults at us every day and to physically attack us. Like silent lambs, we were expected to take it. The moment a Christian was accused of saying anything in response, a powder keg of emotional explosives was ignited.

The attacks on Christians were not just in Gojra. Just two hours north of us in the city of Sheikhupura, Asia Bibi had been arrested for daring to drink water from the same cup as a Muslim woman while working in the summer heat of the scorching hot fields. When the women collectively attacked her Christian faith, unlike a silent lamb, she decided to defend it. As a result of defending her faith against the attacks of Muslims, the crowds were incited to violence and her village was attacked.

A local Muslim cleric announced a reward of five hundred thousand Pakistani rupees to anyone that would kill her. She was beaten, arrested, and put in prison. After a short trial that made a mockery of any idea of justice, Asia was sentenced to death by hanging.

Asia Bibi did nothing more than drink water out of the same cup as a Muslim woman and defend her faith when attacked.

Oftentimes, westerners are told that it is Muslim extremists that create so much death and destruction, while twisting the words or meaning of the Qur'an, but time and time again, it has been proven that it is not the Islamic extremists that demand the death of unbelievers but the everyday Islamic citizens of Pakistan.

My mother's words came back to me, "You have to be a silent lamb. I am sending you out like sheep among wolves." (See Matthew 10:16.) Jesus promised His disciples that they would be persecuted for His name's sake and His promises were contrasted with the promises of Muhammad.

Muhammad, unlike Jesus, promised his disciples virgins and wealth if they followed him. When Muhammad robbed the caravans traveling outside of the refuge city of Medina after he was kicked out of Mecca, just as he promised, he rewarded his cohorts with wealth, women, and slaves. If they died while following him, he had a promise for them too—seventy-two eternal virgins.

Jesus didn't promise virgins or slaves to His followers. He promised them hardship and rejection. He promised that the world would hate His followers because they hated Him first. (See John 15:18.) In direct contrast, Jesus commanded His followers to love their enemies and to pray for those who persecute them. (See Matthew 5:43–44.)

The war of the two promises played out on the streets. The promises of Jesus that His followers would be hated and the promises of Muhammad that his followers would be rewarded if they killed unbelievers.

Young children could be heard chanting in the streets, quoting the Qur'an with their fists waving in the air, "Kill the unbelievers [non-Muslims] wherever you find them, capture them and besiege them, and lie in wait for them in each and every ambush" (Qur'an: Sūrah at-Tawbah 9:5).

They were taught by their schools and families to fight against the infidel and to give their life for Allah by warring against the infidels. Nowhere else were the promises of Jesus and Muhammad more prominently seen than in the children. Muhammad's promise required Pakistanis to die for him, while God's promise was that He would send His Son to die for them.

Jesus's promise was never harder to follow than during the riots. It was hard to follow the command of Jesus and pray for the enemies that persecuted us. It was admittedly hard to pray for anything other than our own safety.

"Our school is not safe. We cannot stay here," Mary continued, interrupting my thoughts. "The church they burned last night also had a high wall and security gate like our school, but it didn't stop the Muslims from burning it down."

Bang! Bang! Bang!

We all instinctively ducked down as distant gunshots rang out. The sound was distant but getting closer. Shafqat ducked his head as if to dodge a bullet, but moving his head was all he could do. If bullets really were to spray through the building, he would not be able to get down on the floor as quickly as the rest of us.

As suddenly as I ducked down, I quickly realized how absurd it was to think that a bullet could make it through the thick brick walls, across the school yard, and into our apartment. It would take more than a stray bullet to penetrate our walls, but the gunshots outside were a sign that the violence was getting closer, and the situation was getting more and more dangerous.

10

THE STRANGLEHOLD OF BLASPHEMY

A group of twelve young girls draped in an array of traditional pleated *patiala salwars* (trousers for females) sat cross-legged on the ground looking down, holding their mouths and giggling. The flowing material made of extra length cupped the wind made by one girl standing up and walking around them.

The young girls were no more than ten years old and made me think of my own little children as I watched them play *Kokla Chappaki*, one of the traditional Punjabi children's games. Like the English game "Duck, Duck, Goose," the little girl standing up, known as the "seeker," circled behind the other girls, stealthily waiting to choose someone to take her place. With a black cotton cloth in her hand, she took long, exaggerated steps on the edge of the small circle of girls until she chose the next girl.

"*Kokla Chappaki Jumeraat aayi…*" she said as she methodically took her steps one after the other, attempting to complete at least one circle before saying the rest. "*Aye jera agge pichey wekhey ohdi shamat aayi aye…*"

One of the girls sitting in a little green dress let out a loud scream before the black cloth was laid behind her and she was tapped on the back to replace the "seeker."

She stood up just as the other girl was sitting down. "*Kokla Chappaki,*" she said, starting it all over again. "It is Thursday today, whoever looks here and there, shall be punished."

None of the girls worried about the violence that was taking place outside of the walls of the school. In the shadow of the cross overhead, they knew that they were safe. The Christians outside of the wall did not have such grand illusions. It was open season on them, and they were terrified. A dark beast lurked behind every corner, waiting to devour them. They kept checking the messages on their phones with the nerves of a skittish cat, waiting for the next outlandish accusation to end their lives.

After an investigation was completed, no evidence was found to suggest that a Qur'an had ever been desecrated, but in the end it didn't matter. In the mind of the collective mobs, the Christians were guilty. If they were not guilty in the situation that they were accused of, then they had secretly done it in private and had not been caught. Or perhaps they thought about doing it. Either way, they were guilty of not being Muslim and that was enough for them to be accused of blasphemy and executed.

Shafqat and I had just brought our children back to the school with the hopes that we could continue the school year without any further events, but tensions remained high. My nerves were freshly torn to pieces, even though the violence had hit a lull. The authorities announced on the news every night that there was no longer any reason for the Christians to be worried about being attacked, but no one really believed them.

One hundred and eighty-five witnesses submitted written statements to the police about the attackers, but no one was imprisoned or punished. Several attackers were identified, but the police did not dare attempt to prosecute them. To do so would have been suicide. Mobs were known to turn on the police, go directly into the police station looking for their victim, drag him or her out in broad daylight, and subject them to Sharia Law as dictated by the local imam.

The Muslim leaders hold the real levers of power. Those holding official offices and carrying the titles of elected officials only hold those positions as the clergy members allow.

A church was burned to the ground, hundreds of homes were destroyed, thousands of Christians had to flee their homes, women and children were burnt alive, and the only thing that an investigation found was maybe the original accusation of some random Christian disrespecting the Qur'an didn't really happen after all.

Everyone guilty of actual violence, terrorist attacks, and murder walked free without a worry in the world. Now the Christians of Gojra were subjected to the swirling leers of predators waiting for an excuse to devour their prey. The system was rigged against the Christians. It wasn't a conspiracy; it was a daily reality. Gojra was a democracy of ten wolves and two sheep voting on what to have for dinner.

Christians knew that their situation was deliberately sabotaged and their voices crying for justice and equal protection by the law were crushed.

"Are you doing okay today, Shagufta?" I heard a low voice say from behind me. I turned and saw Bishop John Samuel looking back at me with his almond eyes peering from beneath his bushy black and grey eyebrows. The bishop had his slight receding hairlines parted to the left. A thick black moustache stretched from corner to corner of his smile, which remained slightly clenched as he spoke.

The bishop could often be seen strolling through the schoolyard in his royal purple button-up shirt and his distinguished white priestly collar with a dark wooden cross hanging from a brown chain that lazily hung between his breast and naval.

"Yes," I responded with very little confidence.

"No need to worry about anything," he said with reassuring authority, asserting that he had everything under control.

"Would you like a coffee, sir?" I asked, smiling at his answer.

"Would it be possible for you to bring me a *lassi*? I heard someone is making them in the break room today."

"Yes, of course, sir," I shot back, bowing my head in honorable recognition of his rank at the school. The bishop was the primary person responsible for getting me the job at the school and I would never forget his kindness.

"Great! And bring it to my office. I am on my way there," he mentioned as I was walking away. I knew that I needed to empty the garbage bin in his office, so the timing was perfect.

A few teachers had gathered around the coffee maker where the *lassi* concoctions were being made. Making a lassi is serious business in Punjab. It is a tangy mixture of yogurt and water and is possibly the most popular drink in Pakistan during the torment of the summer months.

"She was sentenced to death," one of the teachers said while mixing the lassi ingredients in her mug.

"Death?" gasped one of the other teachers. "She is only a girl. She can't be older than thirteen years old."

"I think she is eleven," the first teacher responded.

They were discussing the case of Rimsha (aka Rifta or Riftah) Masih, a young schoolgirl who had just been charged with desecrating the Qur'an. Her case was all over the news and I leaned in to hear more. Like me, the young girl was knowingly born to a Christian Pakistani family. There were early reports of her carrying a bag of rubbish when she was suspiciously asked by a Muslim to let him inspect it. While looking inside the bag, he conveniently found burned portions of the Qur'an. More than 300 Christian families had to run for their lives and hide in a forest outside of Islamabad.

"It is unbelievable that she is facing the death penalty," one teacher exclaimed. "Her parents said that she has Down syndrome!"

"What is the situation with that one lady who was accused of drinking water from the same cup from a well as the Muslims?"

"Asia Bibi?" one of the teachers answered.

"Right! Asia Bibi!"

"Asia Bibi has been sentenced to death!"

"How can someone be sentenced to death for drinking water?"

"It's the extremists. They are after her for speaking out against Islam."

"No!" another woman jumped in with a more combative interjection. "It's not the fanatics! Don't you believe it," she argued. "The majority of the Muslims that I know believe that anyone who speaks out against the Prophet Muhammad should be charged with the blasphemy law. Asia Bibi is not being charged with a law created by fanatics or extremists. It is a law that represents the view of the majority of our nation!"

No one said anything. Agreeing with her too loudly could fall on the wrong ears. Her words were the exact thing that the blasphemy law was created for. If the wrong person heard her, they could accuse her of speaking against Islam and she would be tried with blasphemy.

The room grew quiet, but the woman didn't stop. "People are too afraid to speak out in defense of those who are being persecuted and why wouldn't they be afraid? Everyone who speaks out is either attacked or killed."

She was not wrong. Salman Taseer, the governor of our state of Punjab was killed by his own bodyguard for trying to help Asia Bibi. His bodyguard was heralded as a national hero throughout all of Pakistan for killing the man who was helping a Christian. Three hundred lawyers offered to defend the killer's actions for free. After his execution for the crime of assassinating the Punjabi governor, over one hundred thousand people attended the funeral, and to this day his grave is a sight for Muslim pilgrims throughout Pakistan.

Shortly after Taseer's death, a national assemblyman, Shahbaz Bhatti was also executed by a gunman who opposed his open support of Asia Bibi.

The cases of Rimsha Masih and Asia Bibi were additional signs that things were getting worse for Christians in Pakistan. Not only were women being sentenced to death for bogus charges of blasphemy, but Christians were also subjected to extreme violence and being burned alive.

There was huge excitement in Pakistan a few years ago when Pakistan elected Benazir Bhutto as Prime Minister. Bhutto was the first woman to ever be elected to head a democratic government in a Muslim majority nation. She was a symbol of hope for many women like me that Pakistan was on track to be a more accepting and tolerant nation, but after her assassination, that dream quickly faded.

Now women provided a new symbol in Pakistan—one of blasphemy laws that unfairly punished Christians who did not submit to Islam.

I walked out of the room thinking of Rimsha, Asia, and the future of my own children while carrying a tall glass of lassi in my hand for the bishop. I briskly walked across the open brickyard to beat the clock. Classes were coming to an end, and I would soon need to start cleaning up.

11

A RAID SHATTERS ROUTINE

Watching children come to school was one of my favorite parts of the day. I often spent the early morning hours cleaning and dusting classrooms before the students arrived. About thirty minutes before class, when the children started to trickle in, I would slow down my efforts and watch them. Some would walk in groups while others would meander alone.

The routine of the school removed the fear of the unknown. Schedules gave stability to children and purpose to adults. Agendas, duties, appointments, goals—these responsibilities helped turn off our instincts long enough for us to think about other things that brought us both meaning and joy. I loved routine. It allowed us the feeling of having been there and done it before. Routine anchored me and gave me security. There was a comfort in completing something in the past and everything working out okay; it gave me hope that things would work out again in the future.

Brutal changes were taking place outside the walls of the school. Changes have a way of bringing the fear of the unknown. The children left the unknown of the outside world and strolled into the school with the expectation that normalcy would provide them with the confidence that today was going to be another familiar, unexceptional, typical, maybe even boring day.

The daily solace I found in my routine when I was a child eluded me, but now, looking back, I realized my parents had given me the gift of routine when I was a little girl. There was salvation in the routine of waking up, running to the church for prayers, running back home to eat breakfast, returning to the church for school, playing with my friends, returning home in the afternoon for dinner, and taking care of my daily chores while socializing with my extended family.

At the time I thought I had a boring life, but boredom is a gift for children. The good thing about boredom is that it lacks fear. If it was frightful, it would not be boring. Children should not be living in fear. They find comfort and safety in structure, schedules, and routine. This type of daily routine was the gift that I desperately wanted to give to my children.

The closer the clock drew to the start of class, the busier the schoolyard grew. About 800 children were running back and forth, making sure not to be late. A few teachers straggled behind, swooping up children who were procrastinating with their friends. My heart was beaming with joy as I thought of my own children.

Zain, my first born, was the strapping little man of the house. His skin was lighter and fairer than the other children at the school. His fine black hair parted to the side like a miniature statesman. He was born with a level of maturity that has always given him a calm presence.

Danish, my second son was more curious. His eyes narrowed whenever he studied something that he was not familiar with. He was not always as easy to recognize in the crowds of the other children in the school. He had the round face of a true Punjabi and blended in perfectly.

Next was my sweet Sheroz, who has always been so loving and kind and helped look after my baby Sara. Sheroz and Sara were not yet old enough to attend school, but both very much enjoyed being surrounded by the life of active children.

I loved the end of the school day when I could return to our little apartment room at the corner of the school compound. It was a joy to see my children and feel them breathing in the same room as me.

When the evening came, I stepped away to clean the teacher's break room, but something across the way gripped my attention and broke the string of daydreams I was having about my children. A commotion was building in the area near the staff housing. I could see the guards had left their station, leaving the primary front gate open. The gate was never left open.

Men that I didn't recognize were walking straight into the school without being stopped. These strangers walked with an air of entitlement and passed the guards without permission or showing any papers.

The strangers seemed to have an authority recognized by the guards that was beyond reproach and would not be challenged. It was clear that the guards were more afraid of the men than the men were of the guards.

"Shagufta!" I heard someone yell in the crowd, and it froze my steps. I pretended it wasn't my name and convinced myself that it must have been another name that I heard, and my ears were only playing tricks on me as ears often do when the darkness of night begins to close in.

The idea of returning to my work and dusting off desks in the classroom or preparing the water kettles for the next morning momentarily crossed my mind. Walking into an anxious crowd could be inconceivably dangerous if I were to inadvertently interject myself into a dispute between two parties that didn't involve me.

For a second or two I stumbled as my body moved forward, but my feet had not decided which way to go. I was momentarily locked in the dilemma of not knowing what was going on but not being sure I wanted to know.

"Shagufta!" Again, I heard the word that sounded like my name being shouted out from someone inside the growing mob. I roused myself to look confident enough to maintain an air of innocence.

One of the ladies standing at the rear of the assembly turned and looked at me. I had never seen her before. Her eyes focused on my face and then she turned away, hopelessly enraptured in the emotions of the crowd, seemingly looking for someone.

The closer I got, the less I saw. I was too short to look over the heads of anyone in front of me and all I could see was the broad backs of several strangers that I was certain I had never seen at the school before.

An inner voice whispered quietly, "Turn around and walk away." A warning was blaring in my consciousness. I had never heard that voice before. It was primal and didn't need to be taught. For a moment there was a twinge of unrealistic panic, and I was tempted to turn around and run away—from what, I didn't know.

It was getting late, and the things that I had feared happening to our family always happened in the evening. In my nightmares, it would begin with a sudden jerk out of the bed, violent shaking, and a flashlight beaming into my eyes. I didn't know what I was guilty of or why I had an irrational fear, but it was always there.

Maybe it was the story of Rimsha Masih, the young eleven-year-old girl who was charged with desecrating the Qur'an that caused me irrational paranoia. Perhaps it was Asia Bibi, the mother who dared to drink water from the same cup as Muslims in the heat of the day while laboring away in the fields.

It could be the women and children that were burnt alive in Gojra that caused the fight-or-flight response to rise in me. Whatever it was, it was both rational and irrational at the same time.

Seeing the mob form and call my name made all those nightmares come flooding back. I felt like a skittish deer in the headlights of oncoming traffic, making the situation worse by being erratic rather than calm and still.

"Who is Shagufta?" I heard someone yell out. This time the voice was clearer. I was certain that my mind was not playing tricks on me any longer. It was my name they were shouting. They were now standing outside my door demanding my coworkers identify me.

No one was facing me. They were all facing the door to my home.

I was half tempted to join the crowd and begin asking, "Where is Shagufta?" I didn't feel like myself. I felt as if I was watching everything unfold from a different vantage point at half the speed. Even though they were saying my name, my brain still refused to compute that they were looking for me. I stood at the back of the crowd waiting to see if they might actually find "Shagufta."

"She is not here," came the weak response from an anonymous resident. The timid voice squeaked out like a mouse being squeezed.

"Where does she live?"

No one answered.

"Where does Shagufta live?" came the command again, this time with an unspoken menacing threat reinforcing it. From standing on my tiptoes, I could see that it was coming from an imam, flanked by two police officers.

"She lives there!" someone shouted, assisting the angry protestors.

"That's the one," the imam shouted, pointing out my front door to the police officers. A heavy officer on the imam's left side pushed forward, through the crowd, and with a swift kick of his right foot, kicked in the door. With a violent bang, the flimsy door flew open, and I could hear my four children screaming from inside. There was no announcement, warning, or reason given for their sudden raid. They didn't present any warrants or paperwork showing they had the authority to burst into our home. By Pakistani law, they didn't need to.

My heart immediately started pounding like a drum. I saw the backs and elbows of a group of men as they rushed toward the opening of the door and all tried to fit through the entrance of the threshold at the same time.

I wanted to run in and protect my children, but I was paralyzed, dumbfounded, and beside myself. I was convinced that it was all a dream, and I would wake up at any second. This was merely one of the many nightmares that I had had in the past. I thought, "They can't possibly be looking for me. They can't possibly be looking for me." I repeated the phrase in my head like in a mantra. If I said the phrase enough times, it would all just go away.

"Shagufta! Shagufta!" I heard the police yelling from inside the house. The children were too frightened to answer any questions. From the corner of the door, I could see Shafqat on the floor. They had knocked him out of his wheelchair, and several men were standing over him and yelling.

The banging and clattering of drawers being opened and slammed shut, furniture being flipped, papers being flung, and dishes being ripped out of the cupboard could be heard outside. What they were looking for seemed to be a mystery to everyone.

"Mobile phones? Computers? Hand them over now!" I heard the commands being barked out. A mumbled, unintelligible answer followed, but it was unacceptable. "Mobile phones! Computers! Now! I want all of them!"

We didn't have a computer or laptop. We were too poor. I didn't own a mobile phone. They were growing in popularity everywhere in Pakistan, but I was illiterate, didn't know how to read or write, and mobile phones were simply too expensive for a low wage cleaner like me.

There were no answers to the demands in the house, only screams of terror. The school guards were helpless to stop any of it and the police were accompanying the men that were terrorizing my family. They were terrorists with badges, using fear and terror to get what they wanted.

"Here she is!" yelled one woman to the men inside, tossing the house. "Shagufta! She is right here."

Suddenly, without warning, the colorless face of a demon-crazed police officer charged through the door and came running toward me.

"Shagufta?" he yelled as he ran at me.

"Yes…" I hadn't fully answered before I was tackled and found myself looking up from the ground, thinking that this is how it all must end.

12

BLASPHEMER

"**W**ho do you think you are?" came the savage voice hovering over me. "You are an infidel! You are a motherless dog, and you will die for what you have done."

Suddenly there was leaping, screaming, and shouting from the crowd around me. None of my fellow workers tried to intervene or interject. It was clear that they did not want to provoke them further. A kind of tribal chanting started to synchronize, and the passion of the crowd was growing inflamed. It was not certain which was fueling which.

"Blasphemer!" The word that I dreaded the most rang out.

"No! No! God, please. Don't say that! It is not true," I begged, waving my hands in an attempt to stop them from saying it, but someone yelled it out again.

"Blasphemer!" Now it was more than one person shouting the accusation. It was turning into a chant. The more they said it, the louder it got. The louder it got, the truer it became. My body shook with fear. Even the women in the crowd were baring their teeth as if they were going to consume me like cannibals. Hate swarmed in their faces and uncontrollable exclamations of rage were breaking out in spiritual expressions. The self-righteous imam gripped the emotions of the small crowd like the handlebars on a bicycle and rode their fervor. He massaged their passion by shouting *suwar* (chapters) from the Qur'an.

"I have her ID card!" said one of the young men leaving the house and disrupting the growing chants. He held it up in the air for everyone to see and waved it from side to side in a victorious manner.

"Where is your passport?" one of the officers barked, suddenly looking down on me.

"I don't have a passport, sir," I answered, half lucid of what he was asking me.

"Where is your mobile phone?" he snarled, scowling commands between his gritted teeth.

I was confused and didn't know what to say. Without missing a beat, he yelled again, "Where is your mobile phone? Do not play games with me, you dog! I will not ask you again. I will end your life right here if you do not tell me where it is!"

"I don't own a mobile phone, sir!" I gulped, flinching away from his face, anticipating a smack in the face.

"I told you not to play games with me, you stinking Christian whore. Give me your phone or I will string you up right here in the middle of this school and set your corpse on fire!"

He breathed flames of fiery words that were fueled by his anger. The hate he had for me rolled out of his eyes. Within seconds, his malice raised everyone to a frenzy. People were leaping up and down and shouting *"Allahu akbar"* at the tops of their lungs. Their screams bleated out the further insults the officer was hurling at me.

"Strip off her clothes! Let's show her what we do to blasphemers," someone yelled from the back of the crowd.

"Found a phone receipt!" said another young man, victoriously walking out of the apartment with his prize clutched in his hand. His shout interrupted the calls for my rape. The officer glanced up at the young man with the receipt and then back at me. Beads of sweat rolled down the sides of his face, his shoulders straightened, and his thick powerful chest swelled and stiffened as if he were about to attack.

He pulled back his fist, ready to hit me, and I put my hands out in front of my face, to keep from being hit. Instead, he grabbed my hand, pulled me forward and twisted my arm in such a way that my body was forced to turn away from him and toward the ground. Pain shot like lightning between my shoulder blades. A woman with a dark Muslim head covering over her hair and face shouted behind him, "Swine! Swine! Swine!" She swung at me around the officer, kicked rocks into my face, and made spitting sounds.

Somehow from the ground, I had a line of sight and could see Shafqat withering on the floor of our small apartment. He had been knocked out of his wheelchair and no one was helping him. Above all the noise, the screeching sounds of my children crying out in fear reverberated into the evening air.

"Shafqat!" I screamed. The officer put his boot on the back of my neck and lifted my two arms behind me so high that I thought they would soon snap out of socket. He shifted his heel into my spine and dug in with all his weight. I cried out with such intense agony that I was not able to squeeze out the word, "Stop!" My mouth opened, but I was unable to make any sounds other than high pitched wailing and screeching noises.

"Shut up, you filthy little animal!" I heard someone shout at Sara. She was walking in circles with her arms in the air, not knowing where to go but desperately wanting someone to hold her. The boys were trying to help Shafqat off the floor but were being swatted away like flies by the officers that were in the apartment.

Any pretense that they thought I was a human was now gone. The odious smell of vindictiveness swarmed the schoolyard like a drug that led everyone into a trance. I was no longer a woman. I was not even an animal. I was nothing more than an object of hate, symbolic of all the problems they had in their own lives. Each one of them had turned themselves over to the passionate desire to torture, to maim, to mutilate, to smash my face with their foot, to kill.

I was not even a cockroach to be squashed. I was a disease. A disease is worse than a cockroach. A cockroach can still extract some level of sympathy when it is squashed and killed, but a disease cannot. A disease is always the enemy, and everyone rejoices in its annihilation. Prizes are given to those who kill diseases.

Like war drums beating for the warrior on the battlefield, the officer found strength and motivation from the dark anthems repeated by the angry horde to add more pressure to my neck and manipulate my body in any direction he pleased with the pliability of bubble gum. He moved according to their rhythm and contorted my body in opposing directions. The electric current of venomous hate fed his rage.

He lifted me off the ground as he pulled me to my feet. My feet were not yet under me before he pushed me toward the gate. "Move!"

I tripped and started to fall, but his grip held me up and he continued moving me forward. "I said move!" he commanded again.

"My children!" I cried out.

"Don't you worry. They are going to prison along with you. They will pay for your crimes."

"What crime?" I pleaded again. "I haven't done anything."

"Move!" he demanded again, pushing me toward the gate and out into the street. Two officers ran ahead of us and opened up the back of an old van. My hands were bound together behind my back by the officer pushing me along. With the two doors open I could see a bench on either side of the vehicle. The officer behind me shoved me until my waist slammed into the rear bumper and my face planted on the metal floor of the vehicle.

At that moment the police officer was at one with the will of the people and the will of the people was driven by the *mullah* (a Muslim educated in religious law). There was a mutual cycle of feeding from a circle of perpetual hate. The hate was not ambiguous. It was pointing straight at me. Up to this point I had only been a witness, but now I was a recipient.

"Jesus, help me!" I cried out. Then suddenly, with a sort of satanic stare that one envisions when they rip their head from a sweat-soaked pillow during a nightmare, the officer hissed at me.

"Remember, they hated Me first," I instantly heard the words of my childhood priest quoting Jesus in my ear.

"Mama!" I heard Zain yell. He was surrounded by angry accusers, but that didn't stop the young boy from running toward me with his arms open wide.

"Zain!" I shouted back. At that, all four of my children ran toward the van. They didn't need to be forced to come with me, but the crowd followed them just the same as if they did. A smaller party stayed behind to detain my husband, but I lost track of what they were doing. Holding my children and making them feel safe was all I had the mind to do.

"What is going on, Mom? Why are they doing this to us?"

"I don't know. It will be ok. I promise," I said, attempting to comfort them, but unable to comfort myself. I put my hand on Zain's head and kissed it. Sara crawled up under his arm and wrapped her arms around my stomach.

Outside the van, the crowd split like the waters of the Red Sea as the mullah approached. A Punjabi mullah is a patriarch. The police were doing exactly as he was instructing. They listened intently and eagerly agreed to every word he said as if it were given by Allah himself.

The tan cotton of his long authoritative robe waved from side to side, following the motions of the mullah's hands. He pointed to a piece of paper and then to me and then back to the paper. He then pulled out his mobile phone and pointed back at me again. Each time he pointed his finger, the ire of the police officer grew more and more stark.

In Punjab, the mullah is head of the mosque. They are taught how to read the Qur'an and read in Arabic. Arabic is not the language of Pakistan, but it is a language that rules all of our lives since the colonization of Islam. The mullah was not an Arab, but he was a slave to the Arabic teachings that were branded on him from birth. I was not a Muslim, but I had to live by Islamic law. I was not Arabic, but I was judged by blasphemy laws originally written in Arabic.

Punjabi Christians represent the majority of Christians in Pakistan and can trace their history all the way back to the peaceful evangelism of the apostle Thomas, while Islam came during a time of violent conquest by the Arabs. After the Arabs conquered the ancient Pakistani kingdoms of Makran and Sindh, the traditional religions were forbidden, and Islam was enforced.

After more than 1,300 years, not much has changed. Pakistan still follows rules written in the foreign Arabic tongue, and we are condemned by a language we do not understand.

The mullah looked up, our eyes met, and time stopped. There was a spiritual darkness that swirled around him, and for a split second I saw an evil that I had never seen until that day and may never see again. A black wickedness seeped out from his soul, and a truly dreadful smirk split his face, revealing a cavernous murky shadow.

This was no accident. He enjoyed terrorizing us. I saw the satisfaction in his face. Everyone around him was genuinely angry, but he wasn't. His temper was manufactured in order to terrorize. I watched his smug look linger in his leering glare. It was the look of a terrorist. He was an ordained terrorist.

13

WHAT HAVE WE DONE? PART 2

I was not even certain why I was there. I heard the accusation of blasphemy being thrown around haphazardly, but nothing was certain. In the eyes of the police, I was guilty; the only thing missing was a crime.

"What have we done?" I screamed, forcing the words out with my eyes clenched closed. I had been asking the question since the moment they kicked in my door. I begged them to tell me the entire trip from the school to the police station, but they refused.

"What have we done?" I cried out again. "Please stop. I promise, we didn't say anything against Islam."

"We have the texts you sent from your phone. You think we are stupid? We were able to look up your phone number that you sent the blasphemous texts from," he said in response.

"My phone? But I don't own a phone! I don't even know how to use a phone to text."

"Then how do you think we knew exactly who you were and how to find you?" he snapped back. "We used your phone number from your mobile phone—the one that sent the texts!"

It was all becoming clearer for me now. Somehow a blasphemous text had been sent to the mullah and other Islamic leaders in the area from a phone that had been registered to me.

I did not have a mobile phone and could not use one if I had one. Even if I wanted to send such a text, I would need help from someone else because with only a couple of years of attending a village school, I never learned to read and write. Months before I did have a simple mobile phone in my possession, but it was not a smart phone. It was only for making calls. That phone was misplaced, and I hadn't seen it in months.

"I didn't send a text. You have to believe me," I begged.

The guard scoffed at me, rolled his eyes, and asked, "If you didn't send the text message then who did?"

"I swear it. I didn't send it. I do not have a mobile phone and do not know how to send text messages."

Raising his hand and pointing to the mobile phone receipt that they had found in my house he said, "Then what do you call that?"

"Lying dog!" someone yelled from the hallway as if they were the truth police.

"That is not a phone. My husband sometimes helps repair phones, but I don't know how to even use one! I do not know how to write. Please believe me!"

"So, it was your husband then?" he said, his mind obviously sliding into a world of double accusations where he could catch two blasphemers for the price of one. We were not in the halls of justice, We were in a labyrinth of poorly constructed lies, making a gross mockery of the truth.

The complete law of Pakistan was enshrined in that room, consisting of two opposing truths. This binary nature of Pakistani law confuses foreigners who try to understand it. The two opposing truths of Pakistani law are the written law and the practiced law. One is peaceful and one is violent.

The *written* law of Pakistan clings to the peaceful, pre-Medina side of the Qur'an for the sake of the international community. That is the side that we frame and hang on the walls of our legislative buildings and courthouses for international dignitaries to look at and admire.

Then we have the *practice* of the law. This is the cruel, post-Meccan side of the Qur'an that the true believers actually cling to. This is the side of the law that we see as minority Christians living in Pakistan.

What outsiders do not understand is that Pakistani law is only confusing because the Qur'an is confusing on this matter. The same opposing truths of peace and violence are represented in the Qur'an. One part of the Qur'an advocates for peace and love, while the other demands violence and death.

These two qur'anic truths are knowingly contradictory in Pakistan. However, it caused no challenge for the law in Punjab, at least not for the judge, jury, and executioner in the room with my family and me. They ignored the written law and implemented the traditional law, following instructions also written in the Qur'an.

I had no rights. I was an infidel. I was a minority. My representation was not enough to sway a democracy where the majority of voters are Muslim and believe in the qur'anic teachings that blasphemers should die.

The guards had Shafqat hanging upside down and were beating him. He was receiving Pakistani justice where the guiltless confess to make the pain go away. These actions in turn create false confessions that justify the actions of the abusers.

"Blasphemy! Blasphemy!" chanted the angry imam as he raised his fists in the air.

"Blasphemy! Blasphemy!" replied the crowd gathered in the lobby of the police station.

I knew that my situation was dire enough for them all to wish me dead. The crime of blasphemy was enough to earn the death sentence for Asia Bibi, for eleven-year-old Rimsha Masih to be tried for death, and for young children to be burned alive by angry mobs.

"Please!" I begged, clinging to my children. "Please, we will do anything. Stop hitting my husband."

"Confess!" the guard said, while continuing to beat Shafqat's body.

"Don't you dare touch me, you piece of swine!" the guard said, jumping back as Shafqat swung toward him.

"Ptew!" the other guard spit on my husband.

"*Allahu akbar!*" the guard screamed as he sung his club toward Shafqat's body.

"Blasphemy!" the mob yelled again from outside the room, echoing the shouts of the imam.

"How dare you insult the prophet Muhammad!"

"We didn't do anything," I pleaded. "I swear it. We don't know what you are talking about!" I cried, bowing my head down and shielded my children.

"Liar! We have the text message!" the guard said. "Confess!"

"Confess!" the other guard demanded, but again Shafqat would not utter a word. We were innocent and had nothing to confess to.

"Is he going to confess?" the imam asked impatiently.

The guard turned and looked at him and grimly shook his head.

Stomping into the room, he pointed at me while keeping eye contact with Shufgat. "See your wife?" he thundered, "If you do not confess right now, we will strip your wife naked, force her to walk down the street, and let the men of this city have their way with her and lynch her in front of your children. And I will make sure that you stay alive long enough to watch every moment of it."

I wanted to scream out, "Confess!" but my voice left my mortal body.

"So, you will not confess?" the imam asked.

Shafqat could not confess. I could not speak. We were nothing more than silent lambs.

The imam nodded at the guard, granting him permission to drag my children away from me and hand me over to the mob.

"Okay!" Shafqat yelled out at the last minute.

"Okay, what?" the guard asked, his blood already pumping full of adrenaline at the thought of handing me over to be stripped naked and thrown to the mob.

"Okay. I confess. I confess to everything. I will confess to whatever you want me to confess to," he gulped out his words, barely able to speak. Blood was pouring out from his head and puddling up an inch deep on the floor and spreading out, slowly taking over tile after tile. "I will confess, just please do not hurt my wife."

14

RELIGION OVER LAW

Shafqat's body hung upside down and slightly swung side to side. His head slowly dripped blood onto the ground, plopping drip by drip into a coagulating crimson puddle. The guard with the rubber club that he adoringly called "Hunter" paused.

Shafqat had been beaten with fists, kicks, rifle butts, handgun handles, and rubber clubs. They beat him so hard that they shattered his hipbone into pieces. Shards of bone pierced through the skin and bled down his body, soaking his hair and the floor beneath him in blood.

Instead of protecting the children from such a gruesome scene, the police demanded they watch everything. "Look at what happens when your father is a lying dog!" they yelled. "Learn your lesson, children."

Only when we agreed to confess to whatever they wanted did they stop beating Shafqat. A female officer, strict in nature, began peppering me with questions.

"Tell us who your family members are! What are the names of your mother and father? What are the names of your siblings? What are the names of all your aunts and uncles? Where do they live? What are their phone numbers?"

She was asking so fast and furiously that I didn't know how to answer. My mind was flustered and I was unable to think clearly. When I didn't answer fast enough, she exploded! "You are going to answer my questions, or your husband will get it again—and this time worse!"

She repeated herself again, asking the questions at such a high rate of speed that I was unable to answer one question before she moved on to the next. "Tell us who your family members are, your mother and father! What are their names? Where do they live? What are their phone numbers?"

The questions went on for hours, laced with the howls of more threats.

When they found my brother Joseph's number, they called him and made sure that he could hear us in the background. "Who is this?" they demanded.

"This is Joseph," I could hear my brother answer. They allowed me to hear the conversation as they spoke to him. They asked him where he lived and when was the last time that he had spoken to us on the telephone. When Joseph did not answer their questions fast enough, they slapped Shafqat and made him cry out, ensuring Joseph would hear it.

"Can you hear that, boy?" they asked. "This is what is going to happen to you. We have a police unit coming to your home right now."

They handed the phone over to me. "Talk to your brother," the police officer demanded.

"Joseph?" I screamed into the phone.

"Shagufta? What is wrong? What is going on?"

"Joseph, please help us! We have been arrested and the police are beating Shafqat. You have to help! Please!"

"What is happening?" he asked again.

The police officer ripped the phone out of my hand, put it back up to his ear, "Your sister and brother-in-law are guilty of blasphemy!"

"What? Blasphemy?" Joseph asked, not knowing what it all meant.

"And Joseph," he snarled over the phone, "we are coming after you. Karachi is not so far away. We are coming for you. You cannot escape. We are coming for you and your family."

The police officer threw the phone on the ground and flashed me a maniacal grimace.

My brother Joseph had a great life in Karachi. He had a good job and had really done well for himself, but just being related to me could spell the end of everything for him.

Once I answered all of their questions, they brought in a stack of papers that they had prepared for Shafqat and me to sign. We did as they demanded, hoping to be released as soon as they were done. "This is not a confession," they assured me when they asked for my fingerprint on the paper. "That will come later.

All these papers are a formality stating that you understand the crime that you are being accused of. Once we have that, you will be ready to go back home."

"All you have to do is convert to Islam," the guard said to me after he gave me a tissue to wipe the ink off my finger. I didn't understand. How could he demand that I change my religion? He showed me the paper as proof of my confession. "You have confessed now, and the only way to survive is to accept Islam."

Confession? It was all confusing. They said that they wanted us to confess, but then told us to sign papers that were not a confession, but an acknowledgement. Now they were asking me to deny Christ and accept Islam. I didn't know what was going on. I couldn't even read the papers they were making me sign. "But you said that you would let us go if I signed the papers you gave me," I cried in both disbelief and confusion.

"No. We said that we would not march you through the streets naked and rape you if your husband confessed his crime. We kept our word, but do you honestly think that we would let a rat like you and your husband walk out of here free and clear after what you said about the Prophet Muhammad? Never! Our heads would roll if we were to let blasphemy slide."

I looked at the paper as he passed it off to an administrator who would take the documents off to prove to the rest of the world that they were correct and their treatment of us was justified. That paper freed their conscience. I was not able to sign my name to the confession, so they took my fingerprint on each page of documentation. It was a banner of their victory. An illiterate woman had confessed to a crime of writing blasphemous text messages.

"But we didn't do anything!"

"If you didn't do anything, then why did you confess?" Before I could answer, he answered for me, "You confessed because you are guilty."

"I did what you asked so that you would let us go!"

"A guilty person would not confess just to go home. Where is your honor?"

I didn't answer, but when I looked at him, I saw something that I had never noticed before. I suddenly understood why he demanded that I convert to Islam. In that moment, for a brief twitch in time, I saw a man of honor dedicated to his religion. I understood that he didn't want me to be punished because he had an evil heart and enjoyed watching people suffer. He wanted to see me punished because he was an honorable man of Islam.

His religion demanded loyalty from him, and it was his honorable duty to punish those who dishonored the Prophet Muhammad. A failure to understand this has forever been my failure to understand Muslims.

I desperately wanted to present my side of the story to prove my innocence, but he was not ready to hear it. No one was ready to hear it. No one wanted to hear me argue my innocence, because in some sad way, innocence was a sign of sinlessness and in the eyes of the Qur'an, I was not sinless. I was an infidel. I was unclean and that was fault enough. Listening to me would be a sign pointing to a lack of commitment to Islam and anyone connected to a lack of commitment of Islam was not honorable.

The man followed Islam because that was all he was taught. He didn't know anything else. He did not remember how he became a Muslim. All he knew was that he was. His father was. His mother was. His fellow countrymen were. For him, his actions were a complete sacrifice to Allah and the qur'anic conception of loyalty was unquestionable and unalterable. He didn't need to think. Thought was against his religion. All he needed to do was act. Fear, hatred, pain—these were all emotions that he used as tools against me and my family to show his loyalty. Loyalty to Islam demanded that he show no signs of sympathy, emotion, or deep complex sorrows.

The dark void in his eyes as he spewed venom at me and beat my husband were not his own cisterns of hate, they were wells that had been dug by another generation, and he was left with a bucket in his hands, drawing from the polluted odious springs that had been set before him.

There was only one loyalty in Pakistan and that was loyalty toward Islam. There was no love in Pakistan that came before the love of Islam. There was no art, literature, science, entertainment, innovation, or invention that came before Islam. Only the least loyal to Islam could practice and excel in such things.

For the infidel, there was no distinction between guilty and innocent. We were all guilty and only those who were not loyal to Islam would declare our innocence. Justice for an unbeliever like me only had two solutions and they were the same two that have been passed down since the days of Muhammad—submission or death. Either the infidel will submit to Islam, or they are to be killed. There is no room for investigations for evidence. What good is evidence for the infidel? Evidence of innocence is only reserved for Muslims. The infidel is guilty by nature. The Muslim is only guilty so far as he lacks loyalty to Islam.

Only those showing passion at my demise were true Muslims. Anyone pausing, even for a moment, could be easily accused of sharing in my sin.

Of course, it would be foolish to chalk it all up to religious fervor. Muslims were also accused of blasphemy as well in a bid to obtain power, but the intoxication of loyalty for those wanting to please the God of Islam created the most dangerous scenario for me in that room.

I sat in silence on the floor of the room with my children, walking back through the last couple of weeks in my mind, trying to figure out what went wrong. Our home was raided, we were detained, thrown into the back of a van, and now sitting behind bars at the police station. We were paraded in front of the other prisoners like mass murderers. My four children, disabled husband, and I were not exactly the poster children of a well-organized crime family.

"You see that man right there," the officer said, pointing with his finger. I looked up and tried to see where his finger was pointing. "Right there," he said again, accentuating. "You sent the text to the wrong person. Or should I say, persons."

My eyes must have communicated with him a sign of ignorance because I did not understand what he was saying.

"That man is the most prominent imam in the entire area. He is in charge of the largest mosque." The imam was the one that I had seen barking commands at the police officers at the school and was directing the actions of all of the officers at the police station. "And see that man standing beside him," he continued. I nodded that I could see him. "That! That is his lawyer—that you and your stupid husband sent blasphemous texts to."

I shook my head and gulped down a throat full of shock. Why would that make sense to anyone? Where would an uneducated cleaning lady like me or a disabled man like my husband find the mobile number to an influential imam *and his lawyer* to send a blasphemous text? And why? What would be the benefit of doing it?

We weren't trying to attack anyone's faith. We were trying to survive. I had taken extra cleaning jobs, cleaning the homes of various pastors in the area. Shafqat was taking small jobs. Sometimes he would help the guard shack and keep watch during the late evening hours. He also helped repair mobile phones that had simple issues, which was why we had a mobile phone in our home earlier.

They claimed the phone that had mysteriously sent the text was somehow registered in my name. I had never registered a phone or owned a mobile phone. There were just too many things that didn't add up and didn't make sense, but no one cared to look into it. I was guilty until proven innocent, but we didn't have a chance to prove our innocence.

"I told you!" the imam said, looking at the confession paper in his hand. He beamed with satisfaction, showing the papers to the other police officers. "I told you that I was not leaving this police station until I got a confession," he bragged. The other officers clapped and cheered to affirm his clever ability to intuitively know a person's guilt.

The police officers knew that they could not defy or challenge the imam. Passionate mosque followers have been known to raid police stations in Pakistan, tear down the doors, pull out prisoners, and march them in the streets to death by lynching.

In the Punjabi city of Nankana Sahib, a man accused of blasphemy was not sentenced quickly enough, so an angry mob led by religious leaders stormed the police station using a wooden ladder, scaled the gates, went into his cell, dragged him out, and lynched him in the streets.

A video of the incident circulating all over Punjab showed hundreds of young people surrounding the police station demanding that the police hand over the blasphemer. When they did not, the mob found a way in, stormed the police station with sticks and metal rods, and dragged the man out by his legs into the street. The police were helpless. They knew that going against the local imam would be deadly to both them and their families.

Not only would they lose their jobs, but they might also lose their lives as well.

The police are not in charge, and they do not carry out justice according to the written law. I had only been in jail for a few hours, but I had already learned that they employ the law as seen fit by the religious leaders. The police, just as those whom they police, operate in fear.

15

A NEW HOME: PRISON

The officers silently threaded their way across the room if they needed anything, but for the most part they avoided the room altogether. It was rank with smells of bodily fluids that had started to fester. In the middle of the floor was a filthy liquid mess that had the appearance of vomit, but was a mixture of blood, urine, and excrement from where they had beaten Shafqat.

We had now been at the jail for forty-eight hours and were not allowed to go to the toilet, had not been given food or water, and were physically drained and exhausted. My children were hungry, scared, tired, and dehydrated.

After two days locked up in the police station and watching different shifts transfer duty to new officers, we were finally taken to the courthouse to see the judge. The police separated our family into three separate vehicles. I watched my children taken from me and I protested at first but lacked the energy to put up any real resistance.

My four children were put in one vehicle, I was put in another, and I was told Shafqat would be escorted in a third. I was happy to finally face a judge. My hopes were that he would be able to see that we had done nothing wrong. Maybe our confession would allow us to be fined and sent back home. I wasn't sure. All I was certain of was that I wanted to be back home with my children.

An officer pulled me from the vehicle and walked me into a room where they said that I would be seen by the judge. "The judge will be here soon," the officer said in a low, stern voice. "Don't say a word! You understand me?"

I acknowledged his words with a tired nod of my head.

The judge entered, sat down at the large wooden table elevated high above the rest of the chairs in the room, looked at the papers, and without looking at me mumbled something to the other officers in the room. I couldn't exactly make out what he was saying, but within seconds, the officers in the room dispersed, walking in different directions with speed and purpose.

"What happened?" I asked.

"You have been sentenced to prison," the officer replied.

"What? For how long? What about my husband? What about my children?" I begged.

"Oh, don't worry—your husband is going to prison too!" he said with a psychotic smile.

"But my children! Who will take care of my children?"

"Your children will be taken to a Muslim home and taught to respect the Prophet and Islam!"

I collapsed to my knees in the middle of the hall. The officer tried to pull me up, but I couldn't move. He jerked me harder and when I didn't move, he simply began dragging me.

"They told me that they'd let us go if we did what you wanted us to do! We didn't do anything! We didn't say anything against Islam."

"You had your chance to accept Islam. You didn't take it. Your chances are done. There is no saving you now," the officer said, dragging me to the car.

I didn't get a chance to argue my case to the judge, show any evidence contrary to the accusation, or even get a chance to speak. My husband was beaten till he confessed, and I was threatened with rape and death. We were convinced if we cooperated with the police and signed the reports, we would be allowed to return home. The police told me to stay silent in the courtroom and I thought that it would all go in my favor if I did what they told me to do. If I were obedient and didn't cause any trouble, I hoped that things would work out for the best, but now, the opportunity for me to plead my case had escaped and there was nothing I could do to turn it around.

So many questions were now hitting my mind and I wanted to punch myself for not thinking of them earlier. I never asked if they found the SIM card. I never asked how they connected me to the texts. I only assumed that they were told by the phone company that the texts were from me. I never asked how they knew that the phone receipt they found in my home was from the same phone that sent the texts. I never asked why I was being sentenced if my husband already confessed to sending the texts, even though he did not. I never asked what specific law I was being charged with. I never asked for a lawyer or anyone to provide legal advice.

I was foolish to think that the judge would give me a fair trial. I felt that my innocence would be obvious to the judge, because, unlike the mob at the police station, he would not be influenced by the radical Muslim clerics who wanted my head. I never thought the judge would send me to prison for a text that never came from me. Even if it did come from me, I never thought the judge would send a mother of four to prison for sending a single text message.

I was wrong.

Everyone seemed so scary. I didn't want to be difficult. I didn't want to do anything that would delay the process of me returning home again to my family, but everything I did was wrong. I remained the silent lamb, but instead of being rescued by the Shepherd, I felt as if I was being sent to slaughter.

My innocence was not as obvious as I thought it was. The extreme measures that take place in Pakistan for those who speak against Islam are not just the wishes of the fundamentalists.

Shafqat and I were taken to prison in different vehicles. Shafqat was taken to the general population, far away from me. I worried about him because I had been his primary caretaker for almost ten years.

Not only was he paralyzed from the waist down and required my help for daily tasks, but Shafqat needed medical attention from his severe beating. He needed to see a doctor. His hip was broken, and he had serious wounds that had been unattended for two days while we were at the police station. He had been forced to sit in his own urine and excrement for hours.

I thought about my children, including my baby Sara, who would be without their mother for the very first time in their life. Thoughts of my three boys and what they must be going through ran through my mind.

As they processed me into the prison, I was passed from one station to another as they registered me. I floated like a zombie, without thought or awareness. I was there, but barely. I was the least amount of present I could be without my spirit leaving my body. Nothing seemed real. I didn't know if I could trust my senses any longer.

An officer quietly led me down a long concrete corridor where an open iron gate awaited me. The noise of the prison faded in the background as we got closer.

"This will be your new home," the officer said without emotion.

"Away from everyone else?" I asked, noticing the remote location of the prison cell.

"Away from everyone else. You have been charged with blasphemy. This is a special cell just for scum like you," he said without expression. "Everyone here would kill to have a chance to take your life. Shoot, if they offer enough money, I might even take it."

I shifted at the thought of being killed at the hands of the prison guards. I wasn't safe anywhere—not even in solitary confinement. I could not be placed in general population because the criminals knew that killing an infidel was a guaranteed way to get to heaven.

In Christianity, you are promised heaven when you give your life to Christ and become a believer. In Islam, a person is guaranteed heaven when they take the life of an unbeliever. There are people who would argue with this assessment, but it is not me that they have to convince. It is the Muslim prisoners who believe it that would need to be persuaded otherwise.

The killers, murderers, thieves, and rapists in prison wanted to guarantee their place in heaven and they believed that they could do that by killing me for committing the crime of blasphemy.

Even the prison guards, those sworn to protect me from the others, were now debating whether to kill me or not. One could think that it was only a joke, but Salman Taseer, the governor of our state of Punjab had been killed by his own bodyguard for openly not supporting the blasphemy law. His bodyguard was heralded as a national hero throughout all of Pakistan.

I was given a small cell and put in solitary confinement. I looked around at the tiny space. There was not much to see. The cell was so tight that I could barely shuffle in a circle standing up. I was still in the same clothes that I had on the evening of my arrest. They were the same clothes that my four children had dampened with their tears after hours of crying.

I laid face down on the cot in the middle of my cell and cried out to God. I didn't have the energy to say much. My heart, mind, and spirit were sapped of everything. I was empty. I had been operating for almost seventy hours with no sleep and no food. I didn't have any tears. My dehydrated body had pushed them all out and my tired eyes had none left to cry.

I cried out to God with a silent voice and aching heart, praying that He could hear the words that I no longer had energy to form. I knew that He alone knew my suffering and my challenges. I knew that only He could hear the cries of His silent lamb.

16

THE REALITY OF CONFUSION AND ABANDONMENT

"**S**hut up!" the guard yelled, demanding that I stop crying, but I couldn't stop. I tried to muffle my tears with the inside of my elbow, but the fleshy muzzle was not enough to drown out the sounds of my wailing. I was just starting to understand that I would never make it out of the prison alive. The guards reminded me on an hourly basis that I would die for my crime against Islam.

Of course, they told me that when they first raided my home over a week ago, but it didn't really sink in until they brought me here.

I was not allowed to see my husband. When I asked how he was, the guards would hit the bars of my cell and threaten me with death if I dared ask again. I didn't know if he was dead or alive. I only knew that he would not be able to survive long without medical attention.

My head was throbbing from dehydration and endless crying. I even dreamed about crying. I was not able to escape the pain even in my sleep. My dreams were so intense that I prayed to be awake and when I was awake, I hoped I was still asleep and that I would soon wake up from this nightmare.

"Why are you crying?" the guard said with a clearly disgruntled gruff to his voice. "No one wants to hear you. The best part of your execution will be the final silencing of your complaining."

My clothes had started to ferment in the damp heat after a few days. The prison guards told me that there was no need to give me new clothes because I would be dead soon. I didn't have clean water for washing clothes or even bathing. In the corner of my cell was a rusty pail for going to the toilet, but using it was the same as simply going on the floor. I didn't have to use it often though. The best thing about not eating or drinking for days at a time is that the human body has very little waste left over to excrete. Still, the grimy corner built up over time with the slime of human waste festering in the heat. The smell of urine and feces was the one reminder that someone had been in this cell just before me.

I wanted to see my children. I wanted to hear their voices and hold them in my arms. I couldn't stop wondering if I would ever kiss their little foreheads again.

I might never see my husband again, and I never even got the chance to kiss him goodbye.

The days stringed into nights and nights back into days without any marker of time. I was kept caged up like an animal. After a few weeks, I finally had my first visitor.

"Shagufta!" the guard yelled. I flinched at the sound, knowing that the guard only called my name when he was upset. I didn't remember doing anything to upset him. I had not been crying or praying too loudly, so I was unsure of what I had done to trigger him.

"You have a visitor," he said in a military-style cadence, moving to my cell.

"A visitor?" I thought to myself. I wondered if it could be my husband or perhaps someone who had brought my children to see me!

I couldn't think of anyone else that would be willing or wanting to see me.

I didn't ask any questions. I only followed the guard until I saw the brilliant familiar face of my younger brother.

"Joseph!" I yelled when I saw him.

"No touching!" the guard reminded me. I was ready to run to my brother and leap into his arms. His familiar face raptured me out of the moment and instantly brought me home to my childhood.

He had two other people with him that were there to ask me questions.

"Shagufta!" he said with a loving voice that reminded me that I had not been forgotten.

"It is so amazing to see you! Please help me. Please help me get out of here! Please! I can't stay here one minute longer. I didn't do anything. I swear it. I swear it!"

"I know. I know," he said with desperation in his eyes. "We are doing everything we can, but first we need to tell you what is going on. I really need you to calm down. Please. We want to get you out of here, but we have a lot of things to cover and a very short time. We cannot stay here long, so we have to make the most of the time that we have."

I had so many questions. I had been locked up in a cell for days with no one to talk to. Everyone around me wanted me dead. I had not had an actual conversation with another human being since the day that I was arrested. I had so many questions to ask and so much to say.

"I am so glad you are here to help!" I spoke.

"I didn't have a choice. The police came after me as well. Everyone in our family is being chased down by the police. They want us dead too."

I leaned back, shocked. I had been thinking about my own problems so much that I had forgotten what others might be going through.

"Why do they want to come after you?" I asked. Joseph shrugged his shoulders. "This…" he began to say in a normal conversational tone, but then paused to lower his voice to a whisper, "…this is a blasphemy case. Everyone associated with the person being charged is considered guilty as well."

"That makes no sense. I didn't do anything wrong. You—" I said pointing at him. "You absolutely didn't do anything wrong."

"Doesn't matter. There is mass fear everywhere right now. Our entire family is under attack."

I leaned back again, even further than the first time, wondering what had happened to our parents. I was suddenly reminded of entire villages that were burned to the ground over one false accusation of blasphemy. My mind raced to the families that were killed, the innocent children that were burned alive, and entire villages that had to run for their lives abandoning their homes and livelihoods in order to survive.

"Oh my Jesus, help! How is our mother? Father? Please tell me they are okay!"

"They are okay for now," he said quickly, putting his hand out to hush me.

"No touching!" the guard yelled from a distance, preempting any physical contact.

"But..." Joseph said, retracting his hand to appease the guard, "they are an emotional wreck, as you can imagine. The police busted through the door, raided their home, ransacked every room, and interrogated them. They have been harassed every day."

I buried my face in my hands. "Not Mother and Father!" I cried.

"They are doing better now, but you know they do not understand any of this. You are their eldest child, Shagufta. You have always been perfect in their eyes. They don't know why this is happening."

"I don't know why this is happening," I replied. "I have always done what was expected of me. I have never been in a fight or caused trouble. I have never been in trouble with the law. I am as innocent as they are!"

"This is the first time they have ever faced anything like this, Shagufta. They simply do not know what to do. When the police came, they would not give them any information about what you had been charged with, what they were looking for, or why they were going through their house."

"That is the same with me!" I said pointing at my chest with my index finger. "They wouldn't tell me anything. I still do not know all of the details."

My mother was my best friend. She had been since my earliest memories as a little girl. She knew that she could count on me. When father was sick and no longer able to work, they both knew that they could count on me to help pull the family through. I quit school so that I could support the family. It crushed me to think that they were now suffering because of me.

"Mother has been crying. She is absolutely inconsolable. They have no money to help with any legal fees. They are almost starving as it is."

I bowed my head in shame. I knew he was right. I knew that they could not survive an ordeal like this.

"How are the others doing?" I asked, squinting at how he might answer. I wanted to know, but at the same time did not.

"Not good. When the police came looking for me, I called our brother for help. When he heard what had happened, he said that he is no longer your brother. He disowned our entire family and hung up the phone. He has made it clear that he wants nothing to do with our family ever again."

"Disowned our family?" I shook my head. Not only were my parents losing a daughter. They had now lost a son.

"He publicly denounced you, Shagufta," Joseph said matter-of-factly. "He publicly denounced our entire family and claims that he is no longer related. He said that he no longer has a sister."

"Well. He might be right. He might no longer have a sister."

"Don't say that!" he corrected me right away. "Don't give up hope. There are several people who think that you have a good chance of getting out of here alive. Don't give up hope!"

"How are you doing?" I asked, selfishly realizing that I had not asked anything about his situation. It was clear that he was carrying the burden of the entire family in my absence.

"They came after me too, Shagufta," he admitted, shaking his head. "They called me and threatened to raid my house in Karachi. I reached out to several people for help, but everyone is too scared."

"Who did you reach out to?" I asked.

"I first contacted my church bishop in Karachi. I thought he might know Christians that could help you, but he quickly punted me over to Bishop Samuel at your school."

"What did Bishop Samuel say?" I asked eagerly, knowing if anyone would stand up for me, it would be the bishop.

"What did he say? He wouldn't answer the phone! He put as much distance between you and him as he possibly could. He plainly asked me, 'Where can you go? You need to run away and get out of the country. Go to Sri Lanka—Pakistanis do not need a visa to go there. Just do not call me ever again or attempt to contact me.'"

I was speechless. I could not believe that the bishop would abandon me so quickly.

"I contacted everyone I knew, but no one wanted anything to do with this case. It was too dangerous."

"And we have no money," I replied.

"It wasn't just money, Shagufta. I offered so many lawyers large amounts of cash, but they still wanted nothing to do with it. There were so many lawyers that were angry with me for even mentioning the nature of the crime on the phone. Just talking about it can get you killed in Pakistan."

"But how can this be? Any crime that is committed surely must be discussed."

"Not this! Just mentioning it can get people in trouble. Even now as we come here, we cannot carry any of your court documents with us."

"What?" I asked, not understanding the ridiculousness of the situation. "So, you don't even have my paperwork with you?"

"No. We can't even keep it in our possession, because if someone were to read the words that you are being accused of on the court papers, someone on the bus, or in a taxi, or on the train, or even waiting for the train, we could be charged with the same crime if they reported us!"

It sounded too insane to believe, but after seeing what I had seen in the last couple of weeks, nothing surprised me anymore.

"So, when I couldn't find any lawyers to take your case, I went back to my bishop in Karachi, Bishop Knight. He asked me to join him for dinner because he knew that it was not smart to discuss it over the phone. During the dinner, he promised to reach out and talk to a few people that might be able to help."

One of the men, who had been sitting there in silence, finally leaned forward and said, "That is where we come in."

17

AN INSULT EQUALS A DEATH SENTENCE

The strange man sitting with Joseph spoke with a flat vanilla voice, as if he were reading a menu. His words were complex and mixed with obscure phrases that I had never heard before. He sounded smart, but I was not able to verify it, because I was not educated enough to evaluate it.

The lights of the prison flickered for a moment, which often happened with the unstable electrical supply. The lights were never shut off in the prison. The lack of electricity was the only way that they were dimmed, but it was only long enough for the back-up generator to kick on.

"Shagufta," the strange man said to me while shifting his weight in his seat and placing both hands out in front of his chest to better emphasize his words. His small, slender figure emphasized the professionalism of his pressed and starched black dress coat. He was out of place in the prison. My brother and I fit in with the Punjabi inmates. It was apparent from our appearance that we were Punjabi, but not him. His fine black hair, naturally smooth sanguine face, his moisturized hands and polished fingernails announced who he was before he ever uttered a word.

His eyebrows furrowed, betraying the pity that he had for me, as he continued, "You have done nothing wrong. You cannot be charged with any real crime. You are being held unjustly."

My heart inflated at those words. I didn't understand the other words that he had said, but those words brought me instant hope.

"We are assembling a proper legal team for you now to help you fight this case."

"But how? I can't pay you. I don't have any money."

"You do not have to worry about that. There are people all around the world that have heard about your case, and they are doing everything that they can to help."

"All around the world," I thought to myself. I have never been out of Pakistan. Why would anyone care about me, a cleaning lady from Punjab? It didn't make any sense.

"But how?" I asked.

"We have contacts in other countries that have heard about your case and the way that you and your family have been unjustly treated, and they want to help you."

"What about my family?" I blurted out.

"We are working on the defense for your husband as well and are actively looking after your children's welfare."

"My children? Where are they? What has happened to them."

"They were put in a state foster system when you and your husband were put in jail, Mrs. Kausar, but we were able to find them and have since moved them to be with...."

"I have them now," Joseph interjected. "I was able to get the children." I breathed out a sigh of relief.

"When will I be able to see them?" I asked, looking back at the lawyer, hoping that he would say immediately, but knowing that he wouldn't.

"I can't answer that. First, we need to prepare for your trial. They are charging you with," he shuffled through the papers on his lap and turned it upside down to see it, and then turned it around again, "ah, here we go. They are charging you with Blasphemy Law Sections 295-B, which is insulting the Qur'an, punishable by life imprisonment. Also, 25-D of The Telegraph Act of 1985, which is a maximum of three years for intentionally 'causing annoyance,' and," he paused to clear his throat, "and um...then there is of course, this one which is...."

"295-C," Joseph said, interjecting.

"Yes, Section 295-C of the blasphemy law for insulting the Prophet Muhammad, which is punishable by death."

"I don't understand. How can I be guilty of so many crimes when I have done none of them?"

"Mrs. Kausar," he said, trying to calm me down, but something about the way he called me "Mrs." made me a little nervous. No one had referred to me as a Mrs. before. It was a level of respect that I was not used to and when it was extended to me, it somehow made me anxious.

"We are going to fight very hard for your case. We have friends all over the world and they are ready to help you."

"All over the world," Joseph said, emphasizing that more people were aware of my case than I could imagine. "And we are ready to get them involved to get you out of here and back with your family!"

"Well...now..." the other man said as he put out his arms as if to pump the brakes with his hands. "We have to be very careful."

"But if the world knows that my sister, a mother of four small children, is about to executed over an accusation of a text message that she didn't even send, certainly they would put pressure on Pakistan to let her go. Right, Mr. Hassan?" Joseph retorted.

"It's...actually you can call me Nadeem," the lawyer replied. "But it's not that simple. We must walk a very careful line here. We want to raise the awareness about your sister's case to a level that international leaders know about it and can apply pressure behind the scenes, but we do not want to raise it to a level where there is an international outcry, and the Muslims see this as a Holy War against Islam."

"How would they see this as a Holy War? This is clearly injustice," Joseph argued.

"Not in the eyes of Pakistani religious leaders. In the eyes of Islam, blasphemy laws are clear, and if you insult the Prophet Muhammad, the punishment is death. If European or American governments get involved and publicly put pressure on Pakistan, they will be seen as Christian nations interfering, and the religious leaders will frame this as an attack on Islam. Pakistan is a nation prone to deep distrust and conspiracy theories. Those long-entrenched suspicions intensified after the CIA used a Pakistani doctor to help find Osama Bin Laden in 2011. The informant posed as a worker for an international aid group administering vaccinations. The doctor, Shakil Afridi, was arrested and is being held in a Pakistani jail. When westerners get involved in legal matters or humanitarian aid efforts, the locals are easily persuaded by the religious leaders to believe that it might be a conspiracy.

"Look," Nadeem said, trying to sort out his thoughts. "Your sister's charges are in a long line of recent attacks on Christians. At least three other cases have been registered previously against Christians based on blasphemous text messages alone. In May 2006, Qamar David was accused of sending blasphemous text messages to various Islamic clerics in Karachi. He was convicted in February 2010 and died in prison on March 15, 2011. We don't want that to happen to your sister. In January 2009, Hector Aleem and Basharat Khokhar were accused of sending text messages that hurt Muslims' religious sentiment. They were acquitted of the charge on May 31, 2011. That outcome is more favorable for us. Then there is Ryan Stanton. He was only sixteen years old when he was charged with sending blasphemous text messages in Karachi on October 10, 2012. He has since fled the country after the family's home was ransacked by a violent Muslim mob."

"Wow!" I cried after hearing that. The situation was suddenly becoming clearer. It was not just me. This was a series of attacks that were being hurled at Pakistani Christians. The entire country was seeing attacks, riots, burning of churches and houses, executions, and the slaughter of small children. Even political figures were being assassinated. The problem was bigger than I had ever imagined.

Nadeem then looked at me, and his eyes narrowed in on my face as he continued, "The complainants are what really gets me here," he said, shaking his head. "First, we have the grand Imam Muhammad Hussain, who is arguably one of the most influential religious leaders in Punjab. And then there is a lawyer, Anwar Mansoor Goraya, who is not just any lawyer. He is actually the president of the entire bar association. Together, they are the worst people that anyone would ever have imagined to send blasphemous texts to. It seems a little too convenient for me, that these two were the ones to get blasphemous texts from a poor, unknown cleaning lady living in the corner shack of a Christian school." Joseph slammed his fist into the wooden counter in front of him, making one of the guards jump and take a few steps in our direction.

"Our time is almost up, Mrs. Kauser," Nadeem said, looking at his watch. It felt like we had only started. I was only just starting to understand the situation better. I couldn't believe that the time was already over. "I am working on your case together with a Christian NGO. They are a Christian charity group helping raise awareness about your case, but the situation is very tricky for us. We are in a very precarious situation. Just a couple of years ago, Muslims who did not like the idea of a Christian ministry working in Pakistan during an earthquake relief effort sent men armed with grenades to attack our offices. They killed six of our colleagues—four men and two women."

I gulped a breath of sharp air and covered my mouth in shock. "Oh, wow. I am so sorry."

"It was a brutal and senseless attack," he said. "Christians are not the only targets in Pakistan. Any Muslim who helps Christians are also targeted. So, on this case, we want to try and maintain a low profile. We are going to need Muslims to help us if we are to succeed. We want some media attention, but not a lot of media attention. It is a 'Catch 22,'" he said using a phrase that he could see I didn't understand the meaning of.

"Catch 22," he said, explaining, "We need media attention so that high officials will put pressure on their counterparts in Pakistan, but we don't want too much media attention, because that will anger Pakistani Muslims and make everything worse for everyone."

Nadeem looked at the confusion on my face. "I know that this does not make a lot of sense to you now, but trust me, it is the right way to go forward with your case."

"Time's up!" the guard on the far wall yelled out.

"Stay strong," Joseph said as he started to stand up and leave.

"Wait!" I cried out instinctively.

Joseph paused and looked down at me with eyes that expressed the obvious question, "What?" I had nothing to say. I only wanted to suck out the last second of my time with the only human beings who did not want me dead.

18

THE INJUSTICE SYSTEM

"Shagufta Kausar!"

I heard my name shouted outside the corridor and stood up. I could hear footsteps coming closer but couldn't see who it was. Keys jingling and metal clanging were always the precursor sounds before a guard came to my cell to retrieve me.

"Let's go!" the guard said, opening the door to my cell. After living in the squalor of a solitary cell, I was finally taken to my official court hearing.

A few moments later, I saw Nadeem, my lawyer I had met earlier, waiting on me. Then beside him, I saw Shafqat. "Shafqat!" I screamed. I almost took off in a sprint and leaped into his arms. I had not seen him in months and desperately wanted to hold him.

"No touching!" the guard shouted and his authority stopped me in my tracks.

Shafqat smiled and swallowed back his tears. He hugged me with his eyes and slumped in his wheelchair, staring back at me. Our eyes were glued to each other. I was unable to look away.

"Shagufta," Nadeem said. "I have been talking to Shafqat and have gone over the defense with him." Nadeem looked over at me and noticed that I was not looking back. I couldn't take my eyes off Shafqat. It had been so long since I had seen him last.

"The last time we saw a judge, you were not allowed to say anything," Nadeem continued, realizing that getting my full attention might not be possible.

"Yes!" I said suddenly snapping back into reality. "There are so many things that we are being accused of that simply aren't true. They can't be true. The judge will understand that as soon as he sees how ridiculous they are when he hears our side of the story."

"Wait!" I said, suddenly wondering why we were not being taken to a car or going to the courthouse. I turned and looked around and saw that there was a seat for me in the hallway of the jail. "What is this?" I asked confused.

"This is your seat during the court proceedings," Nadeem said, adjusting my chair without looking at me.

"Huh? My seat? What does that mean?"

"I am sorry, Shagufta, but your case is too dangerous. We have to do the proceedings here in jail. Getting you from here to the courthouse is too much of a security risk. There are people throughout the city that want you dead. The courthouse can't provide enough security for you, me, the judge—no one. Listen, these cases are a hot issue right now in Pakistan. Writing texts against Islam is more of a threat to Muslims in Pakistan than suicide bombers. Three more Christians in Lahore have been charged with blasphemy since you have been here. One of them, Pastor Adnan Masih is being charged for simply pointing out the errors that were made by a Muslim scholar when misquoting Christian teachings in a book called *Mein ney Bible sey poocha Qur'an kyun jaley* or 'I asked the Bible why the Qur'ans were set on fire.' Pastor Adnan is a scholar with a master's degree and wrote comments beside parts of the book with the correct biblical references to correct the errors made. Nothing blasphemous was written, except the corrected Bible verses in the book's margins!"

"The judge is coming here," Shafqat said. "The trial will be held here at the jail."

"Ok. Phew. I thought that it might be like last time where we had to stand before a judge and not speak," I said with a sigh of relief.

"Well…" Nadeem stammered. "You will not actually be able to see the judge, or rather the judge will not be able to see you."

I looked at Nadeem dumbfounded. "What?"

"For security reasons, you will not be able to be in the room while the trial is taking place."

"What security reasons."

"Security reasons," Nadeem replied, not knowing what else to say. "You and Shafqat will sit here, and you will be able to hear everything.

"But how can we see from here," I asked, stating the obvious. It was impossible to see anything from the vantage point of the hall.

"You will be able to hear everything, even if you can't see," Nadeem answered. "But unlike the last time, I am here for you. I will be your eyes and ears and more importantly, I will be your voice."

"The honorable Judge Mian Amir Habib has arrived," the guard announced. Nadeem shuffled his papers, put them in his leather case, and walked away. Before he was completely out of sight, he turned and smiled at me and put two of his hands together making a quick symbol for prayer, indicating that he wanted us to pray.

After Nadeem passed from view, I tilted my head to hear better. The sounds in the other room echoed down the long windowless hall with its staggered guards and closed wooden doors. The echoes were chopped into small bite-size segments by the hum of distant voices, scooting wooden chairs, and shuffling papers.

"Good morning, your honor," I heard someone say. It was the first sound to break through the cacophony of random kinetic noises. "I am representing the complaint of Mr. Muhammad Hussain." I looked up and noticed that I could see part of the makeshift prison courtroom through netting that draped down to separate the rooms.

"Good morning, your honor," Nadeem followed. "I am representing the accused, Mr. Shafqat Emmanuel and Shagufta Kausar."

The introduction was followed by more paper shuffling and several people asking for different forms that I had never heard of before. With all the new voices, it was difficult to follow over the noisy distractions and being so far removed from the people talking. The concrete hallway bounced sound in a way that made everything audible, but not understandable.

"On July 21, 2013, last year, your honor, a case was brought against the defendants for a blasphemous text sent to Mr. Muhammad Hussain that insulted the Qur'an and insulted the Prophet. The text was shown to several witnesses. When the police inquired about the text, the text was confirmed to be sent from a SIM card in Mrs. Kausar's name."

"Your honor?" Nadeem interjected.

"Not now," the judge barked. "Continue," he said, indicating for the prosecutor to continue speaking.

"Thank you, your honor," the first lawyer said, clearing his throat. "Presented as evidence to the court is a copy of the text and…" There was a short pause again, followed by more shuffling in the room. I remained as still as I could to hear everything.

"These texts are in English letters," the judge pointed out.

"Yes, they are, your honor. We did not want to offend the court by presenting the translation as evidence."

"So, the text was sent using English characters?"

"Yes, they were, your honor, and if it pleases the court, please note that shortly after the complaint was filed, the police found evidence of the phone in Mrs. Kausar's home. She and her husband were arrested, and her husband confessed to the crime of sending the blasphemous text."

"Say something!" I shouted in my head to Nadeem as if he could hear me. I was trying to send telepathic signals to him to speak up and speak out. I don't use English letters to write in Urdu. I don't speak English. They never found a mobile phone in my flat. They didn't find a SIM card, which is why they were saying they found "evidence" of a SIM card.

"Your honor!" Nadeem interjected again but was quickly squashed.

"Blasphemy is waging a war against Islam and the Qur'an, and the Sunnah demands death to those that wage war on Islam!" someone shouted, which started a random launch of Qur'anic verses from all around the room.

"This cannot go unanswered! The law is clear what should happen to those that blaspheme against the Prophet!

"Blasphemers shall have a curse on them: whenever they are found, they shall be seized and slain without mercy [Qur'an: Sūrah al-Aḥzāb 33:61]," one booming voice said, quoting the Qur'an.

A momentary hush fell over the people in the makeshift prison courtroom. I could not see through the mesh netting what they were looking at or what had calmed them.

"If this court does not bring justice," one voice said to the silence of everyone else, "then the duty will fall on the people. We will all be called to be Mumtaz Qadri!"

Mumtaz Qadri is the martyred bodyguard who assassinated the Punjabi Governor Salman Taseer for his stance against Pakistan's blasphemy laws as they were implemented against the peasant farmer woman Asia Bibi. It was a direct threat to the judge.

The people cheered, indicating that there were more people in the room than I had assumed from the beginning. I couldn't count them all, but I was certain they were more than those that had a direct part to play in the court proceeding itself. My life was in the balance between life and death, and I was not allowed to even be in the room, but my accusers had a direct audience with the judge. They were able to look him in the eye and threaten his life and the lives of others with impunity.

Nearly everyone jeered for my demise, proving that though the masses might find comfort in numbers, they rarely do what is right. The majority can be right, but if they are wrong, it is the minority that suffers. There is safety in numbers, but for the minority there is death.

"Thank you for the support of this court," the judge said with a beaten little voice, squeaking from his chair, as he capitulated to the petitioners after they threatened him.

"I object, your honor," Nadeem said in a deflated tone that carried no authority to be recognized at all.

The judge continued to thank everyone in the courtroom and announced that he had reached his decision. He excused himself and stepped away to retire to his makeshift chambers.

And just like that, everything was over. The only thing that they were waiting for now was the verdict. The judge never reviewed any of the evidence against the accusation. He never allowed us to refute the evidence presented against us. He didn't even ask the lawyer if I was guilty or innocent! It was a sham. I was never supposed to win.

I felt so defeated that it was hard for me to even pray. My lawyer did not get to challenge any of the bogus evidence against us, and I was not able to stand before my accusers and refute their accusations. It was not a real trial, but more of a show similar to *Ainak Wala Jin*, the one I used to watch on our black and white television when I was a little girl.

Within minutes, the judge returned to the room. I heard the commotion of multiple indistinguishable conversations lower to a whisper and then the scuffling of furniture as people sat back down in their seats.

The judge was ready to read his verdict.

"Shagufta Kausar, in accordance with Article 295-C of the Pakistani Penal Code, the court sentences you to death by hanging and a fine of three hundred thousand rupees."

19

A BROTHER'S DETERMINATION, COMFORT, AND KNOWLEDGE

"**B**ut he didn't say anything!" I cried. "We are innocent, and I'm not allowed to say anything to the court in my defense. If I take my defense to the rest of the world and plead my case, the government gets angry and threatens to kill me. If I remain silent, I will be sentenced to death and the government will kill me. What am I supposed to do? Why didn't our lawyer help us make a case?" I was allowed to have a few minutes with my brother before being taken back to my cell.

"I do not know. It seems like he is just as helpless as we are," Joseph said. "I will continue fighting for you, sister. You must remain strong."

"How can I remain strong when the entire world seems to be against me? I have been charged with a crime that I do not fully understand. Do you?"

Joseph slightly shook his head, evidently showing that he had learned a few things in his late nights with the various lawyers and human rights activists. He looked around trying to determine if he should keep silent or tell me what he knew.

"Please tell me what you know, Joseph. You are my only connection with the outside world. You are the only person that can really help us."

"Blasphemy is a law that is common among Islamic nations, but the international community does not like to discuss it, especially cases like yours."

"Why?" I asked puzzled.

"Because…" Joseph hesitated, trying to look for the best way to describe it. "I am not sure exactly, but it seems that the international community wants to pretend that this is a shared problem among all the nations in the world."

"But it's not. You just said that blasphemy is a law common among the Islamic nations. Right? So why not say it?"

"I don't know. Maybe they don't say it for the same reason that we don't even mention it here in our own country. Do you know what I mean?"

"Kind of," I said, trying to follow along.

"Look, I can't bring your court papers into a public space. Why? Because just seeing those words on paper can enrage Muslims to the point of violence. We know it is wrong. We know that we should have the right to carry court papers with us. For goodness sake, we are fighting for your life—yet we do not dare carry them—even to save your life! Why? Because those papers have the potential to incite violence."

"What if the international community is doing the same thing?" he continued. "What if they are like us? What if they know that blasphemy laws are wrong, but they do not want to discuss them because to do so will incite violence? Why would nations want to stir up the anger of Muslim nations?"

"Do you think they have to deal with the same violence that we deal with here in Pakistan?" I asked.

"Of course they do!" he responded back. "Look at the cartoons of Muhammad in Europe. There was violence in the streets. Entire cities were burned. Those were only cartoons! Nothing more! They were not harmful to Muslims. In fact, the cartoons elevated Islam to be accepted in the same public forum of European culture as Christianity, Buddhism, Hinduism, and other religions by treating them as equals. The cartoonist was simply saying that Islam is familiar to them, and not a stranger. More than two hundred and fifty people around the world were killed during those riots...over cartoons!"

I sat, stunned at what Joseph was unpacking. He had learned a lot from his time with the human rights agencies that were trying to help me.

"It's not just you, Shagufta, who are dealing with this. And it's not just me. It is the whole world. The international community is living in fear and tiptoeing around the situation, hoping to find a peaceful solution to the problem.

"Why didn't you speak out against your accusers when they kicked down the door to your home?" he asked me.

"Because I didn't want to inflame the situation any further," I answered.

"And why did you agree to confess to a crime you didn't commit at the police station?" he asked, apparently finding a rhythm to his line of thinking.

"Because I just wanted to go home. I didn't want any more trouble."

"And why didn't you confront the judge who sentenced you to death? What would he have done to you for speaking up in court? Sentence you to death again?"

"I thought things would be better for my family and I if we could just quietly slip away without causing more outrage."

"Exactly! And that is the entire world right now. The entire world is acting as if everyone is under a prohibition against speaking out against Islam to not upset the Muslims and as a result they are not facing the real problem. They are too afraid to even mention it for fear that it will cause more problems or encourage more violence. They are trying to appease the child in the room so that he will not explode into a tantrum."

Joseph looked at me and got closer as he talked. "There are hundreds of people that are charged with blasphemy all around the world every year. One human rights group told me that those cases all come from forty different nations, but the number one nation that charges people with blasphemy is Pakistan."

"Really?" I asked.

"Yes, Shagufta." When Joseph used my name like that in conversation, I knew he was about to say something important to him. I could tell that he was getting passionate.

"Pakistan is one of the oldest and largest civilizations in the world. We have the world's largest deep seaport, Gwadar, the world's highest paved road—one of the eight wonders of the world! We run the world's largest volunteer ambulance service to help the sick. We are the only Muslim nuclear power. We have the highest mountain ranges in the world, the world's only fertile desert, and we made history by electing the youngest female prime minister in the world."

I shook my head trying to follow as he continued. "Does any of that matter when we lead the world in senseless deaths, killing minority women and children for barbaric and defenseless blasphemy laws?"

"And what is blasphemy? Is it a cartoon in Denmark? Is it a scholarly pastor defending his faith from an unfair description? Is it a mother working in the fields trying to get a drink of water from a cup that she is too unclean to drink from? Or is it a mother of four with a disabled husband trying to survive by cleaning classrooms who is falsely accused of sending texts in a language that she can't write with and a phone she doesn't own? Is that blasphemy?

"In the United Nations today, Pakistan is leading the effort to implement blasphemy laws and they are doing it in the name of silencing 'hate speech.' By ramping up the rhetoric on the perceived threat that has been labelled anti-Islamophobia, they are effectively convincing free nations to close their eyes to the real problem and ignore persecution against Christians."

The idea that the world was willing to ignore or even adopt the same brutal laws that have sentenced me to death was unthinkable. Only fear could push such an agenda. By closing their eyes and allowing blasphemy laws to be relabeled as anti-hate speech laws, it really did appear as if the international community was nursing a viper that would one day bite it.

"Preventing humans the right to accept or deny religion does not increase freedom, it takes it away. A person is not Islamophobic just because they dare question the mysteries of Islam. It is better to have questions that cannot be answered than answers that cannot be questioned. The criminalization of 'blasphemous' expressions does nothing to protect human rights but is the key to ripping them away. Pakistan wants to force other nations to protect Islam, while at the same time ignoring every other human right known to man that has been agreed upon by the United Nations."

"But what can be done? Pakistan is its own country and can make its own rules," I said, pointing out the helplessness of the situation. However, my brother did not see things as being helpless. He felt that there were plenty of things that the world could do to stop the injustices in Pakistan.

"Actually, the world is not helpless. If they were not afraid of standing up for the minorities, they could point out that Pakistan is a signatory to the United Nations Universal Declaration of Human Rights (UDHR) Article 18."

"Wow! Now you are speaking jargon that I do not understand." I could tell that he had been spending time around lawyers and discussing things that I had never heard of before. Saying phrases like "Article 18" highlighted my ignorance on this issue.

"There is nothing complicated about it. It simply states that, 'everyone has the right to freedom of thought, conscience and religion,' and that, 'this right includes freedom to change [their] religion.'[1] Pakistan has signed that law and has agreed to abide by it."

---

1. United Nations, Universal Declaration of Human Rights. https://www.un.org/en/about-us/universal-declaration-of-human-rights.

"But what can other countries do if Pakistan does not keep their word after agreeing to it? It seems to me that their hands are tied, no?" I asked.

"No! There are many things they can do," he said confidently.

"Like what," I inquired again.

"Trade is huge for Pakistan. Pakistan currently enjoys free trade with the United States and the European Union and this nation's economy would crumble if that was ever taken away. These nations could easily put an end to the violations of human rights by using these tools. They have a lot of power, but they are too afraid to use it."

My hands were trembling as Joseph was speaking. He was putting into words all the things that I had been thinking but had been unable to express.

"It's sad that the world is silent. These atrocities are happening every month in Pakistan and nations are too afraid to speak out. They are afraid of the violent repercussions," he said, shaking his head, looking down to the ground as if hoping to find the answers there.

"I heard that there was another Punjabi Christian arrested for allegedly sending a blasphemous text," I said, curious if Joseph had heard anything in the news.

"Yes, I have heard about him. His name is Pastor Zafar Bhatti. It is almost the same story as you. He was arrested several months before you were and is in prison facing the death penalty under Pakistan Penal Code Article 295-C."

Now that I had been charged with Article 295-C, I felt that I heard it everywhere. Pakistani Muslims were using it like a sword against all their enemies to take jobs, land, steal money, or cleanse areas of Christianity.

"Pastor Zafar worked for a small medical company in Punjab and launched Jesus World Mission, a small NGO[2] to help the poor. Just like you, a local Muslim leader reported that Pastor Zafar sent him a text message insulting the Prophet. The problem with the accusation was that there was no connection between Pastor Zafar and the phone number that the text originated from. There was zero evidence! Just an imam lodging an accusation, a justice system too afraid to look at the evidence, and an international community too afraid to cause trouble by speaking out too loudly against the injustice."

"What happened to the pastor?" I asked, hoping to hear that his case was dropped and, in some way, giving me hope that the same fortune would eventually happen for me.

"He denied the accusation but was tortured until he confessed. There was a woman that was also accused—same as you. The greedy judges try to maximize the pain from the shady cases to satiate the hunger of the masses that desire to see Christians killed whether they are guilty or not. Her name is Ghazala Khan, and she was arrested on the same charge as Pastor Zafar and now they are both facing the death penalty if they are convicted of blasphemy."

"Time is up!" I heard the guard say. He moved toward Joseph to lead him out of the visitor room.

I looked at his face as if it would be the last time I ever saw him again, because I knew that it very well could be.

---

2. Non-government organization. These non-profit charity groups operate independently of government influence.

I was ushered back to my lonely cell where I sat and endlessly pondered all the things that Joseph and I had talked about. His words kept circling around in my mind. The thing that kept coming back to me was how Pakistan has so many other issues, but this one is one that they choose to focus on.

Pakistan has serious food shortages, people dying of hunger, economic woes, health care deficiencies, lack of electricity, assassination of politicians, military coups, and instead of trying to make things better on those fronts, they choose to focus on shady blasphemy accusations. As Pakistan grows more Islamic, it tends to put more energy on adherence to Islamic law than human rights or economic development.

20

NEVER FORSAKEN:
DEFEATING LONELINESS WITH HOPE

I heard rumors about Pakistani prisons. I no doubt formed pictures of them in my mind from things that I saw on television or heard in stories. I imagined prison yards, mess halls, metal showers, rusty sinks, and mass uncontrolled fights.

The luxuries that I imagined, saw, or heard about didn't exist where I was holed up. The idea of strolling in a prison yard seemed extravagant. Instead, I was locked up 24/7 in a cell so small that I could stretch out my arms and touch the side walls. The thought of having access to a rusty sink instead of a dirty bowl of water that I had to make last for days was another denied extravagance. I longed just to have a toilet, instead of a modified hole in the floor that festered in the corner by where I slept. It all seemed like a dream that I could rarely conjure up to indulge in my imagination.

I faced horrors untold. Not many books are written about the prisons in Pakistan, and I do not recall seeing any movies made about them. Many of the people that go in never make it out to talk about the hellish conditions. The stories are hidden deep with the corpses that are unable to talk from their buried graves.

I was locked in a solitary cell and the key was thrown away. I was tossed in and forgotten. My cell would keep Pakistan's secrets safe for a moment, and my grave would keep them hidden forever.

The other inmates were fellow burial vaults. I couldn't recognize them, and I didn't know their stories. As long as they remained nameless and faceless, their stories would remain voiceless. I lacked the ability to identify other inmates or even myself. When the fellow burial vaults saw me, they didn't know my name. They didn't know my story. They only knew my title: blasphemer.

Blasphemer indicated the worst kind of crime—a thought crime. The religious leaders in Punjab didn't just want to control my actions but wanted to control my thoughts. They couldn't, so that is why I had to die. They could control my actions through laws and fear, but only for a time. In the long run, if they could not control my thoughts then soon, they would no longer have control over my actions. I didn't understand that before, but I do now.

My thoughts were not influenced by the Qur'an, but by the Bible. This threatened almost everyone that passed by my prison cell. There was this irrational fear that I could infect their mind at any moment. If I could infect their mind, then I could change their thoughts, and if I could change their thoughts, then I could influence their future actions.

The prisoners guarded their minds by reminding me that I was nothing. The prison guards reminded me that I was nothing. And if I ever forgot, my death sentence reminded me that I was nothing.

Solitary confinement is where the nobodies are sent to be forgotten and rot until they die. It is a quarantine to ensure that no one else is infected with the disease of free thought. In my solitary cell, days and nights smashed together into one unrecognizable blob. I was not able to tell one day of the week from another.

I remember how much I would look forward to Fridays when I worked at the school. We all rejoiced at the thought of a break during the weekend, but in my small cell, there was nothing to break up the monotony. I dreamed with my eyes open to escape. I dreamed of a glossy world where I was free to live and love my family. Over time, I created scenarios of having a good job and a healthy husband. I closed my eyes and wished to be somewhere else, anywhere else. My dreams entertained me as I built them up, block by block.

I squeezed out every ounce of faith that I could muster with the hopes that I could wish my dreams into reality. I'd pray to God to allow me to open my eyes and see a world created in my dreams.

My dreams were not unrealistic. I didn't dream of fancy mansions, fame, or extravagant shopping trips to Paris or New York. I wasn't asking for world domination. My dreams were simple. God didn't have to expend a lot of miraculous energy on my dreams. They could be granted with His leftover power—the power that He wasn't currently using anywhere else.

"Grant to me, oh Lord, to return again to the village that I love," I would say with a smile and my eyes closed. In my mind, I left the sounds and smells of the prison behind. No longer was I in a rat-infested prison with women crying and the smell of my own urine festering beside my bed. Instead, I was in my father's yard, cooking beside my mother. In the same instant I was walking along the small alleyways behind the village shops, selling spices and vegetables. I could hear Jackey-Jackey barking as he ran beside me on the way to church. In that cell my mind transported me to the sights, sounds, and smells of my small apartment, in our warm bed at night, hearing my children breathe in and exhale out.

Reality punched me in the face, demanding that I recognize it, but I squeezed my eyes tighter and hung on to my dreams. I wanted to live in my dream just a little longer. I didn't want to come back. I wanted to believe that Jesus would transport me out of that cell. "I can have faith, Jesus. I can have the faith to leave this place!"

Eventually the prison would drag me back by my feet, forcing me to open my eyes again, and reality prompted me to confess that Jesus didn't answer my prayer. I was still in prison and without hope.

Pakistani prisoners get used to living without hope. I didn't have a job or work to keep me busy. All I had were my dreams. Before prison, I spent every day doing something industrious from the time that I woke up until the moment I lay down to go to sleep. I have had a job since I was a little girl. It was torture for me to sit and rot in a cell and do nothing all day every day. I had nothing to do and no one to talk to.

The only things that hadn't forgotten me were the rats. The putrid smell of the toilet hole in the ground brought in large black rats that scurried about in the night, biting my feet and ankles. I would try to sleep with my knees in my chest to keep them from biting off my toes.

The closest people that I had to talk with when I was in prison were the visitors the guards would bring to my cell to taunt me. "You see her," they would say in a taunting manner. "This is the woman that dared defame our prophet."

"This is the woman?" they would say with inscrutable scowls of disgust. They didn't see me as a human. I was something foreign and alien to them. In Pakistan, children are taught at a young age that Christians were lower than dogs. I was lower than an animal, so it would only seem natural to them that I was in a cage and on display like an animal in a zoo. Now they could actually see me in the flesh. I was the embodiment of their boogeyman.

I despised them and longed for them in the same breath. I loathed their peering at me as if I were an animal at a zoo. I detested the platform they gave me, placing me on a perch to point at me as an image of repulsion, but deep down they brought human contact and reminded me what it was like to be around people.

My days were numbered, and I didn't have much more time to live before I was executed. I desperately wanted to connect with another human being. I didn't want to take the long walk with the only memories behind me being from a jail cell that was more like a dog kennel than a prison. I desperately wanted to make a friend and to have human contact.

I longed to hear another voice besides mine or feel touch from someone who loves me. Being alone was one thing, but I was more than alone. I was lonely. Solitary confinement taught me the difference.

Throughout the years, I had chosen to be alone. In fact, there were times that I preferred it, but loneliness is spiritual. Loneliness isn't just the absence of people, but the absence of love and acceptance. Loneliness is the knowledge of the absence of Light and the ever-present shadow of darkness. People can be surrounded by others and be lonely. They can be alone and be completely unaware they are lonely, but when they are made aware, then it cuts the deepest. Loneliness is heavy and oppressive.

I knew what it was to be loved, so the loneliness was perhaps greater for me than it might have been if I had never been loved at all.

"You do realize that everyone in this prison wants to kill you," one guard said to me shortly after my trial. He leaned against the wall right outside my metal door and looked at the dirt under his fingernails. His long rounded nails protruded out from his middle and index finger. He turned his hardened palms inward and examined each of them. They were stained with black crud, like that of a mechanic or grave digger.

He continued talking to me as he evaluated his nails. "Some of these prisoners have nothing in life left to hope for, but you," he said with a cackle in his voice, almost joyous at the thought, "you give them hope."

"I give them hope?" I repeated to myself, proud that I might have served a purpose in prison. I jubilantly shouted in my own mind without moving my lips, "I am a Christian! I have the hope of Christ inside me. Of course I give them hope!"

The guard could see that I was satisfied with his comment and immediately sought to remove it. "Don't look so happy. The hope you are giving them is not the kind you think. They all want to kill you, and your death gives them hope. The thought of killing you gives them hope. Now they have something to live for." He leaned away from the wall, let his hands down and looked directly into my cell. "Now they want to stay alive for no other reason than just to kill you. They do not want to eat. They do not want to sleep. They do not even want to die before they get their opportunity to kill you!"

He sucked the life right out of me. He knew it and was proud of himself. Just for good measure he added, "We have prisoners in here that could not wait for their execution day. They were miserable, and worthless with no purpose in life, but now they have purpose. Now they do not want to die until... they get a chance to see you die."

"How does killing me give hope?" I asked, not able to look up but knowing he was still standing there with a commanding presence over me. The dirty fluorescent light noisily flickered above his head.

"Look at me!" he commanded. "Look at me or I swear I will come in that cell and slap the life out of you. Now look at me."

My eyes slowly scanned up his leg, then his torso until I saw his flaring nostrils and steaming eyes. Anger mixed with the hypnotic power of control over another human being clearly intoxicated him. "I will educate you…snuffing the life out of your body will guarantee my entry into heaven because you are an enemy of Islam. A thief, murderer—even a rapist will be warmly welcomed into heaven if they kill you. Allah will hold the door open and roll out the red carpet for bringing justice to the world by removing you from the face of the earth."

His hate was impregnable. Any act of kindness to me would have been an act of rebellion against his faith. Mercy was a thought crime and betrayal of the Qur'anic teachings.

"I like you, Shagufta. You know why?" he asked with a grimace, but I didn't look up. I couldn't listen any longer. I felt completely defeated. "I like you, Shagufta, because you give us all hope."

I sunk my head down, but I was not defeated. I was alone, but no longer lonely. Something shot through my veins and reminded me that Jesus had not yet abandoned me. I might die, but they couldn't kill me. They couldn't kill what has already died. I was crucified with Christ and was already dead. It was not I who lived, but Christ who lived in me (see Galatians 2:20).

Suddenly His holy words that I was taught as a little girl came to me. *"For he hath said, I will never leave thee, nor forsake thee. So that we may boldly say, The Lord is my helper, and I will not fear what man shall do unto me"* (Hebrews 13:5–6 KJV).

The guard looked at me. His eyes bulged and he stepped back with a reverse shuffle. He lost his balance. The spirit in him was not stronger than the spirit in me. I was in prison, but his prison was worse than mine.

He persisted, regained his stability, and grabbed the bars of my cell, muscling his way back up. "Look at me," he commanded again, but this time he did not actually have to say it. I was already looking him in the eyes. This time I didn't see hate or anger. I saw primal fear.

"Accept Islam and all will be forgiven," he said, gulping for breath. "Deny Jesus and the judge will let you go. They already told me. It is simple. Just say, 'There is no god but Allah and Muhammad is his prophet,' and we will let you go to see your children again. You can return home."

"You can't give me what you do not have," I replied. "You can't offer me freedom. I already have it. You cannot offer me life. I already have it."

I could tell that he didn't understand a word that I was saying, but he felt the power of what was being said. The words bubbled up from a place that I never knew was there. There was a part of me that wanted to jump at the chance to be released from prison. I would have been a fool not to want to leave. Everything in me desperately wanted to be home with my children, and now I was being offered an opportunity to have it. It was within my reach.

This was not the first time that I had been offered freedom in exchange for accepting Islam, and it would not be the last. I no longer felt alone in the prison cell. Knowing that Jesus was with me took away the death pit of loneliness.

21

A GENUINE, SAVING KINDNESS

"I have some tea for you, Mrs. Kausar," said the sweet voice from the other side of the door. I didn't respond. I had stopped eating. I had been fasting and praying without ceasing, and now I didn't know if I had the energy to eat anything. I was desperate to hear from Jesus.

"Jesus," I pleaded. "Please hear Your daughter in my time of need. Don't forget me. I am desperate to hear from You. I need You now more than ever. Do not forget me in this wretched place."

"Mrs. Kausar?" came the sweet voice again. "I have roti, vegetables, and sweet rice."

"It must be Monday," I thought. The food schedule was the only thing that separated the days. On Mondays the prison served sweet rice, vegetables, and flatbread. On Tuesdays, they brought *gram dal*, which is a split chickpea, rounded on one side and flat on the other. It was served with flatbread. Wednesday was the same gram dal that wasn't eaten on Tuesday, mashed together and served again.

Thursday and Saturday were the same as Monday, with vegetables, rice, and flatbread. The spacing out, every other day, helped to distinguish one day from another.

Fridays were white *gram*, a Pakistani type of legume, served together with flatbread.

"You must be hungry. You haven't eaten for over a week. It is not good for you," she said, softening her voice even more, ensuring the guards couldn't hear her. She swept back her slate-stone hair that was hanging loosely around her left eye so she could see a little better. She blew upwards when it swung back down again. Her lips tightened when she talked, so other inmates could not see her mouth move.

"You know," she said, starting a confession with her lips still pursed together, "you remind me so much of my daughter. You are a lot like her. I have not seen her in many years." A mixed sadness suddenly descended on her as it does with most mothers in prison when they start to think of their children. I didn't know her daughter, but her large dark eyes expressed the heart of a mother longing to see her daughter again.

Suddenly, I was standing beside my own mother, looking up at her from the warm heart of a tandoori oven buried in the ground, absorbing the last gilded rays of the evening sun. My dreams of being a mother and a child were intermingled and not fully divisible. The landscape of being a mother to a child was often a reflection of the love felt by one's own mother as a child. Somewhere between the time of suckling and being suckled stands a woman thankful for being a mother while hanging on to the feeling of being a daughter.

I never outgrew my mother's love, just as my children will never outgrow mine. The world sees a blasphemer, but my mother only sees me, the face of her little girl.

I looked over the door of my cell and saw the woman's round face and almond inset eyes gazing back. In my village, I would have called her "aunty" out of respect. Many of the elderly women look after the children of the village and are called "aunty," even if they are not an actual blood relative.

Her kindness won me over and reminded me of the Bible verse that says *"the goodness of God leads you to repentance"* (Romans 2:4 NKJV).

For days I had been fasting and praying, begging God to not forget me, His daughter. I didn't want to eat again until He answered my prayer. "Please hear Your daughter in my time of need. Don't forget me."—This was my prayer, and my prayers were interrupted by a woman carrying food to break my fast who said I reminded her of her daughter!

No doubt God used her to remind me that I was not a forgotten daughter.

I took the tin bowl of flatbread and rice from her and bowed my head low in gratitude. "Thank you, Mama," I said. It was bold to call her mama, but it felt right to both of us in that moment. Her presence on the opposite side of the iron bars was a soothing ointment bringing healing to my soul.

"I am also imprisoned here and work in the kitchen. I noticed that you have not been eating, and I am worried about you, child. A grown woman needs to eat."

Like a healing balm, her words were a direct answer to prayer. She was the first sign of hope that I had seen in prison since I had arrived. There was no reason for her to treat me with such love and kindness. She had nothing to gain and everything to risk.

I didn't know if she was Muslim or Christian, but it didn't matter. Her kindness was genuine, and it felt good to be treated like a person again. I looked up to heaven and thanked Him for hearing my prayers. I knew that He had not abandoned me.

"You are looking a little yellow, child," she said, evaluating my hands and arms. Tearing a bite from the chewy flatbread, I glanced down and back up to compare my arms to hers. She was right. I had turned several shades lighter into a greyish tint of lemon. I kept chewing, trying to not give it too much attention, but it was clear that my body was suffering from malnutrition.

The thought suddenly hit me that I didn't know what I looked like. It had been so long since I had seen a mirror that I was unaware of what my hair or face looked like. Were they just as ashy yellow as my hands and arms? I had been living like an animal for so long that I had forgotten what it was like to own even a tinge of vanity.

"Slow down, child. I don't want you to choke," Mama said with a light chuckle. "There is more where that came from. If you would like more food from the kitchen, I can bring it."

"Really?" I asked, wondering how she had so much freedom.

"Yes. It's easy, really. You see over there?" She said pointing with her finger further down the corridor. "My cell is right there, not far from yours. I pass your cell every day on the way back to mine."

She turned and looked behind her to see if anyone was coming. She relaxed a little more and spoke with a more natural voice when she saw that no one was around. From the inside of my cell, I was not able to see if anyone was coming or going. All I could do was listen.

"I have walked by your cell for over a week, and I could see that the guard brought you food and sat it on your door," she said, using her head to point to the small slot under my prison door window. "But when they came back to retrieve the plate of food, it was as full as they had left it.

"I just knew," she continued, "that it isn't good for a young woman to starve. You must eat."

"I didn't know if I wanted to eat. I think many of the people here would prefer me to not eat. They could get rid of me quicker."

"Don't say that child! You have children at home that love you. They need you. You are their mother. You have to survive. You can't give up hope. You are the only hope those four children have."

"How did you know I have four children," I asked, completely surprised she spoke about my family with such confidence.

"I work in the kitchen, my child. I hear things."

"What kind of things?" I asked, my curiosity piqued.

"All kinds of things. If there is anything happening in the prison, you can be certain that the kitchen is the first to know."

"Are all these women accused of blasphemy?"

"No, just you, my child," she said with sadness.

"Then why are they here?" I could think of no other reason why so many women would be imprisoned. "Were they here for murder, theft, bootlegging, or...?" I didn't know how many types of crimes could lead to a woman being imprisoned.

"Many of them are here for crimes that they were forced into."

"What does that mean?" I asked curiously.

"It means that Pakistan is not kind to young girls," she said in a defeated tone. "You see that girl over there?"

I squinted my eyes trying to see, "That one there in the dark, greenish saree?"

"Well, yes, her too, but I was referring to the woman just behind her," she replied. I squinted a little closer and saw a woman hunching along with a long dark grey *patiala salwars* with a murky maroon border.

"Take a closer look. Can you see her face?"

I tried to make out her face, but she had most of it covered with fabric that slightly draped over her head.

"I can't. She is covering it."

"Exactly. You will most likely never see her face. She hides it. She was a Christian like you. She was only eleven years old when a Muslim man saw her walking home from school and decided he wanted to marry her. One day, after class, he followed her home and kidnapped her. She was forced to marry the man and convert to Islam."

"I've heard about this," I said, explaining how my mother warned me to not travel to town alone.

"Your mother was right to warn you. Young girls are kidnapped from school every year in Pakistan by older Muslim men and no one does anything about it."

"It's accepted?"

"Well, it hasn't stopped. The government will say they are against it, but they do nothing to the men that kidnap and rape the young girls. Thousands of girls have been kidnapped like her," she said pointing back at the woman covering her face. "Once they are married to a Muslim man, they are no longer allowed to have connection to their own parents."

"Why? That sounds horrible!"

"Why? Because they are Muslim and after converting to Islam—even if by force—they can't connect with their parents because they are Christian."

I almost vomited from the disgust and injustice forced on young girls in Pakistan.

"So, she was forced into marriage?" I asked, curious of what that had to do with her covering her face.

"Yes, but she was able to escape and return home. When her husband found her after she escaped, he threw acid on her face. It melted the skin clean off. Her eyelids? Gone! Her lips? Peeled off her gums! Now she must live the rest of her life with the face of a monster. Shame too, because she is one the sweetest women you will ever meet."

"But why is she in jail?" I asked. It didn't make sense. Was getting attacked with acid a crime? "It would seem to me that the man that attacked her should be in prison, not her."

"No, he is free. He was never charged with a crime, but when her parents reported that their daughter was kidnapped and raped, the law required her parents to produce four male witnesses that saw the rape take place. When they couldn't produce the four witnesses, their daughter was charged with adultery. She is now serving a life sentence in prison for sex outside of marriage."

I almost vomited again.

"Sick, isn't it?" Mama said. I nodded my head in disgust. "She's a brave one. Most women don't ever make it to prison. They commit suicide long before they are sent to prison. Do you remember Mukhtar Mai?"

I shook my head. Her name sounded familiar, but I didn't know from where.

"She is a Punjabi woman whose brother had an inappropriate relationship with a girl from another clan. As a punishment for his sinful behavior, village leaders ordered his sister, Mukhtar Mai, gang raped. She didn't even commit a crime—but was brutally raped by six men. Her body was used to punish the sins of her brother!

"Young Christian school girls are kidnapped and forced into marriage almost every day here in Pakistan and if they try to fight back, they are brutally attacked. If they turn to the police, they are thrown in jail. If the family of someone is guilty of a crime, it is their young daughters that are humiliated by rape or worse."

"I know the feeling," I whispered under my breath.

"How?" Mama asked.

I perked my head up, alerted by the fact that she actually heard me. "Yes. My husband was ordered by the police to confess. The Islamic leader, together with the police officers that were beating him, told him that if he did not sign a confession, they would parade me through the streets naked and I would be raped and then lynched. He confessed to save my life."

Mama shook her head. "I have heard it all too often. Just a few weeks ago, here in Punjab, there was a five-year-old girl whose body was dumped outside of a hospital in the city of Lahore. She had been brutally raped until her little body couldn't take any more and the attackers thought she was dead."

"That's horrible!" I thought of my own little Sara who was the same age. "Did they arrest anyone?"

"The news said that they found several suspects but had to let them go—because they didn't have four witnesses as the law requires."

I could hear the shuffle of footsteps that sounded like a guard making their rounds and checking the cells. Mama looked back and saw someone coming.

"Now remember what I told you," she said, going back to her whispering voice. "Keep eating. If you need more food, just ask."

"Ok, Mama," I replied.

"You don't belong here, child. If I get out early, I will tell others about you. I will not forget you!" And then, as she walked away, she paused, turned, and said, "Jesus is with you."

22

LESSONS IN THE CONCRETE

I once thought cracks in concrete were ugly. Their imperfections break the patterns of the contractors' perfect parallel lines and wreck otherwise flawless symmetry, but now I envied them. I lay on my back, hands folded across my chest, and I followed their jagged lines to freedom. They go where they want and cannot be stopped. Years ago, when my cell was being constructed, the concrete form was planned and poured with the hopes that there wouldn't be any cracks, but the cracks didn't ask for permission. They came and they left. They entered my cell and left their craggy rigid trail as they exited.

I followed the cracks as far as I could, but they went further than my eyes could see. Each crack had a story with its own personality, direction, and shape. Did the crack first form outside of my cell and then come in through the ceiling, or did it start inside and then leave?

This wretched Pakistan jail could not imprison them. The cracks on the ground are trodden underfoot, every day, by both the prisoners and the guards; they do not die, they breed and advance. If the master adds to their load, they do not buckle, they grow.

The cracks in the concrete withstood the blazing sun and the monsoon rains. When dry, they imitated art, and created hundreds of images that danced in my imagination. Sometimes the cracks went up, down, and around in the shape of a car, house, or head of a cat. There was one crack in the corner of my cell that, if I looked at it just right, resembled a watch hand pointing to four o'clock.

In the rain, the cracks didn't fear. They drank what they wanted and were never thirsty. The paths of the cracks reminded me of life. They were never straight. They never went from point A to point B in a single line. It was difficult to tell why the cracks took the paths they did. Did they take a different path for the scenery? Did they need to learn lessons along the way? Were they confused, not knowing that going straight was the shortest distance?

The crack in my cell didn't have a name, but that day it was my only companion. My mind had no other thought, my cell had no other visitor. I was desperate for a companion and incapable of finding another. Mama had not stopped, so the cracks were my guests. No one else welcomed them, but I did. I strained my eyes to see them more clearly and attempted to count them, but there were too many. My feet did not leave the prison on that day, but my mind escaped on a journey following the concrete crack in my cell.

The crack spoke to me and influenced my morning prayer. "Use this crack to take me away from the house of the oppressor, my Lord. I beg Thee. Your Word is a lamp for my feet and light for my path. Though it is jagged like a crack, may it continually go in the direction that You have set for me. Though my journey has many ups and downs, unexplainable twists and turns, I pray that Your will be done on earth as it is in heaven. My cup of oppression is overflowing. My enemies feast on my misery. Write again my story. Do not let it have this ending, oh Lord."

Laying in the bed and following the cracks took my mind off the circle of daily life where everything was repeated. My mind was dying the slow death of dreary numbness where nothing changes, not even the cracks on the wall. The cracks escaped to exciting places, but their irregular patterns in my lonely cell remained the same.

Eating, urinating, and defecating were the three activities that marked the hours of my day.

Sometimes I would play a game in my mind by listening to sounds outside my cell and guessing who or what made them. If I heard keys jingle down the hall, I would say to myself, "Those are keys bouncing off the hip of a guard that had them tucked away on his belt loop. He was heading to Mama's cell to let her out. Today is her last day in prison. She is going to leave the prison and tell the governor of Punjab about me. He will feel so sorry for me that he will issue me a pardon and I will be released and can go home."

Soon after, I would hear boots shuffling. "Oh...I know this one!" I would say to myself, "Those are the polished black leather shoes of the head female prison guard. She is walking in her drab green uniform, the shiny rank insignia on her shoulder flickering in the light, cotton pants swishing with every step making her way to conduct the inspection of her employees. She wants to see that the uniforms of her female officers are pressed, and they are treating the prisoners with respect. When she sees how badly I have been treated, she will apologize, issue me a pardon, and I will be released to go home.

"Bang! Bang!" Now I could hear the metal cart making its way down the uneven corridor toward my cell with loudly clanging dishes bouncing off each other with every bump. This was not a part of the game that I needed to engage my imagination for, because it made the same sounds every day.

The meal schedule had changed since I was transferred to Jhang Prison. Jhang Prison is in the center of the Punjabi city of Jhang, on the east bank of the Chenab River. I didn't know much about the city of Jhang, other than it was not a very big city. The prison itself was like its own village with over 1,700 prisoners. I was told that we had a drug rehab center, vocational training, library, store, and medical facility, but I would never get to see any of them. I would only ever see the inside of my solitary cell where I was confined away from the rest of the population.

The meal cart was pushed by a prisoner and escorted by one of the guards. The rattling sound stopped when the cart would pause every five feet to deliver a plate of food to a prisoner.

When the cart approached my cell, the prisoner and guard were very careful not to touch me. The tray was very carefully put on the shelf window that was crudely cut and welded into the metal door. I was like a disease. No one wanted to see me or touch me in the prison. It was like my death sentence for blasphemy was stamped into my forehead.

I lost my connection to Mama when I was transferred to Jhang Prison. I had no friends in prison or allies that I could count on.

"God, I come to You again! I feel alone and abandoned. I need Your Word to give me strength." I prayed for hours every day for God to give me release from the bondage that I had found myself in.

After several months at Jhang Prison, God answered the prayers of many women when they were released. Pakistan extended amnesty to many mothers who had been serving long prison sentences and allowed them to return home to their families.

I was not released, but instead was transferred to another prison called Multan Women's Prison. "Multan will be your final home," one of the transportation guards told me before the two-hour ride south.

In many ways, Multan Women's Prison was completely different from what I was used to, and in many ways, it was the same as all the other jails in Punjab. The facility was in a more rural area with far fewer prisoners. There were many women there for murder. The other inmates were serving time for drug-related issues or prostitution. Some were charged with kidnapping, a common charge for abused women who try to escape with their children.

Some of the women at Multan Prison were allowed to have their children with them. The thought of having my children with me in prison was not ever entertained. I was not a common prisoner but was on death row. I was also in prison for blasphemy—a crime that the Pakistan government did not want to be passed from one generation to the next.

Hearing the laughter or voices of children in the prison quickly took me back to my own. The guardians over my children did not allow them to come and visit me.

I thought of Zain. He was my big boy. I bet he was even taller than me by now. I prayed that God would protect him and lead him and his brothers Danish and Sheroz. I could see Danish's little face now, running to give me a hug with Sheroz running closely behind with outstretched arms with his fingers in the air.

I wanted to scoop my little Sara in my arms and squeeze her until I couldn't squeeze anymore.

Something terrible happens when a mother is separated from her children. Although prison is no place to have children running around, the argument can be strongly made that it is better to be with their mother than to be with strangers or in an abusive home. There is a long-term traumatic effect that echoes through generations when children are not with their mothers. I have seen children suffer acute emotional and developmental problems as a result of being ripped away from their mothers.

Most of the women were uneducated and illiterate like me. They were typically young, poor, and came from disadvantaged economic backgrounds. They didn't have money for lawyers or anyone to even read to them their charges.

These women were often accused and prosecuted without a fair trial. I didn't get a chance to meet many of the women in the prison, but those that I saw seemed to be products of abuse.

Some suffered from mental health issues. The prisons were no place for them, but here they were.

They didn't know about the legal rights of women in Pakistan and were therefore vulnerable to some of the vilest tormentors. Most of them had never heard of the Constitution of Pakistan passed in 1973, which promises equal rights to all citizens, including women. Written in black and white, the law repudiates discrimination based on sex, and affirms steps to ensure full protection of all women in all spheres of life, even when protection is needed from the government that has sworn to protect them. All Pakistani citizens are equal before the law and are entitled to equal protection of law, or so it is written.

The law is written for equal protection, but in reality, the women in this prison have been largely deprived of their legitimate rights. Those in power can be blamed. Culture can be blamed. We can even reach back 150 years and blame it all on the colonial rule of the British—as if that has any impact on how we govern ourselves today. The true culprit that few are willing to admit to is Islam. The example that Muhammad gave his people, the customary practices found in the Hadiths and the Qur'an, and the unequal power structure for women are all contributors to the situation for women in Pakistan. The same disgusting practices from Muhammad's rule on the Arabian Peninsula remain largely unchallenged in Pakistan today.

When I was in Multan Women's Prison, just as in the other prisons, I fell to my knees and began to pray. More times than not, I begged God for His protection, but this time was different. I often begged Him to allow me to see my children or to go home and let the world forget about me. I desperately wanted to hide in my little corner of earth and bask in the safety of anonymity, but He had other plans.

My dark nights taught me to pray differently. I was illiterate, but my tears learned to write a new history for my future. My fate would not be decided by the slaves of sin. I would blaze a new path to bring light to the darkness and life to the dead. Truth would be written on the walls of this prison for every forgotten soul to find hope.

The defeat of a long, dark winter when the trees stand dormant and no field can be harvested was proclaimed, but it was a false report. My spring winds were rediscovered under the dead leaves of autumn. My hopelessness was replaced by the joys of Christ. My death sentence was traded in for a life of purpose. He had given me the power to transform a cursed situation into an undying testimony.

The fire of the Holy Spirit burned bright and illuminated my path, which I had been unable to see before. I tried to light the flame, but I could not. I didn't have the resources. I tried to create the flame, but I was not strong enough. Instead, I learned to be a lantern for the flame. I would house the flame and allow it to burn inside me.

My life might be soon snuffed out. My lantern might soon be destroyed, but the fearful gusts of Islam would not extinguish the light of God in my lantern, because His Flame burns eternal.

"Father, allow me to pray the way that You taught me to pray. May Your will be done, not mine, on earth as it is in heaven. May You use me. If You can use anyone, please use me."

23

NIGHT VISION

"**W**ake up!"

I opened my eyes and strained to see who spoke to me but all I saw was the empty night's blackness in front of me. Lifting my head, I sat silent and listened for a few seconds or a few minutes—I do not know which as I lost all track of time. I tried to look for shadows or any line that might indicate that there was someone else in the cell with me, but there was nothing.

The lights of the prison were always on, but tonight there must have been a power outage because I was not able to see anything in my cell.

I laid my head back down on the meaty portion of my forearm that I was using as a pillow when I heard it again. "Wake up and pray!"

I shot back up again, sitting so high on my cot that I felt the warm evening air hit my face. The prison was silent and sullen with sleep and the sun was not to rise for another three hours.

"Wake up and pray!" The words echoed in my head. I listened for the footsteps of the guards. The prison security must have heard.

"Wake up and pray!" echoed the words again. This time, I rolled off my cot to my hands and knees and crawled back to the makeshift altar of my cot. The dusty floor stained my hands and knees, but I didn't care. I was solely focused on the words that played in my head over and over: "Wake up and pray."

I didn't know how to pray or what to pray for at that moment, but the Word of God illuminated my mind, and I prayed as I was led. A soft, humming sound played in my head, strumming the chords of my spirit. I was awake now, both physically and spiritually.

I now knew that I was not alone in the cell, even if I couldn't see anyone. Like the jagged broken cracks on the ceiling and walls, the steel mesh of my cell could not keep the Holy Spirit out. The horizontal metal bars and steel door prevented anyone from going in or anyone from going out, but Jesus had a key to unlock all the doors.

I silently prayed, "Lead me, dear Lord. I am here. I am Yours. Tell me what You want of me." I pressed my hands together, interlacing my sweaty fingers. The evening brought temporary relief from the burdensome heat. A sweat bead fell down my forehead and clung to the far corner of my right eye. The saltiness burned for a moment, but I blinked, and the pain dissipated.

As I prayed, I heard the sound of my thoughts, and it occurred to me that I hadn't awoken from the voice of a guard or dream. I awoke from the voice of the Lord calling on me to pray.

I prayed harder.

I felt a shaking in my body and did not know if it was me or the ground below me. The metal hinges of the massive steel door did not make any vibrating noises, so I concluded that it was me. My hands vibrated in rhythm with the beating of my heart.

My faith grew in my prayer. It began flexing. I felt as if I was kneeling directly in front of the cross, and Jesus could hear every word. I had His ear, and He had my full attention. I was in fellowship with Him. I was on my knees, but I was climbing to heaven. With every word I was getting closer to the throne room of Jesus. I could feel His presence so strongly that I was moved to tears. Nothing else in the world mattered except being with Him.

I could feel myself straddling this world and the next. The guards were asleep, and their ears couldn't hear me, and the cell bars couldn't stop me.

"Jesus!" I cried out. I felt Him beside me in the prison cell. I heard His voice, "Get up and pray." I could not see Him, but I felt His glory. I could not touch Him, but that did not mean that I could not feel Him. He was silent, but I heard His voice playing over and over in my head.

My eyelids were clenched shut, but they had never been more open. I could see! I could see that the Lord was using me, and that Satan wanted to destroy me. My prayers illuminated my mind in a way that I had never experienced, even in church.

I felt power, unexplainable power. As I prayed for things, I could see them happening in my mind. I could see the future transforming its shape to change into what I prayed. I visualized the future according to my prayer.

Not only could I see the attacks of the enemy coming at me in the future, but I could also see them in detail. I saw the imam that came to my house. His hate filled me with strength, and I pitied him. He was blind and enslaved. I was watching him as if I was viewing him from the sky above, and I could see that he was completely powerless and afraid.

As I continued to pray, I could see the face of the police officer that arrested me and took me to jail. He was a tool being led and guided by a force that he could not see. He too was a mere slave, shackled with the chains of the lies of Islam.

I closed my eyes and looked out again and saw the judge that sentenced me to death. He was a detainee and had no power to give me death or life. His hands were bound behind his back and his feet were chained to the floor. He wore two sets of manacles. The ones around his ankles were the Qur'an and the ones cuffing his arms together behind his back were Sharia Law.

The judges that sentenced me to death were all helpless victims. Like sock puppets, they had no control over their actions or emotions. They had no control over their hate. They were poked and prodded by the enemy until they did what they were required to do. They did not have any choice. They lived in constant torment, enslaved from birth.

Suddenly it was revealed to me that in the moments that I felt weak, I was made strong. The judges felt strong, but they were pitifully weak. I felt like a victim, but I was shaped into the victor. I was a prisoner, but I was free. They felt free, but they lived in bondage.

The judge, police officers, the imam, and the prison guards didn't have my freedom. They all felt free, but they were inmates. They thought they were deciding things for themselves, but they weren't. They were being played like fiddles. Every indictment they threw at me was predetermined. Every word they used to condemn me ripped away their own freedoms. Every attack they launched to make me weaker, subtracted from their strength. They sentenced me to death and signed their own death warrant.

"I understand, Lord," I cried out. "Now I understand."

On my knees in prayer, I could feel a warmth on the right side of my body that felt like the body heat of another individual.

"Jesus?" I called out into the dark air. There was no answer, but I knew I was comforted. His presence revealed things to me that I had never seen before.

That night transformed my life forever. I never looked at my prison cell the same way again. I knew that I was more than a conqueror in Christ. Not only did I feel it, but the guards could see it. They could see that something was different about me than they had seen before.

"Could you pray for me?" one of the guards asked the next morning. I almost fell out of my locked cell. One of the guards who used to taunt me and falsely accuse me of things that I had never done was suddenly asking me to pray for her and her family.

When I prayed for her, I suddenly understood things that would happen to her in the future. Words flowed out of my

204 Under Threat of Death

mouth, as I prophesied over her in a way that I could not control. The words simply flowed out of my mouth with power and purpose. I have always been shy and short on words, but something new had been conceived inside of me, and I was giving birth to a new role.

Suddenly, in my prayers I could actually see the future shaping while the words flowed out of my mouth. I could see what was going to happen next in someone's life. It was directly connected to prayer. Visions began to play out, and I prayed with them instead of for them. I was not creating the future, but agreeing with the will of God as He created the future and allowed me to witness it.

My life transformed into one of continual prayer. I woke up again many times in the middle of the night and prayed in the silence of my solitary cell. One night while praying, I saw the main wall of the prison fall down. It collapsed in front of my eyes as if the ground under it gave way. People were lined up around the wall, crying. When I looked closer, I could see that my children were there with the people at the wall, and they too were crying.

"Wait a minute," I said as I looked at the wall. "This is not the exact wall of the prison."

"No, this wall is your security," said a faint voice in my soul. "Death is coming."

When the vision ended, I prayed for strength for whatever came my way. I knew that someone important to me was about to die, and I needed to be ready for it. "You and You alone are my security, Father," I prayed. "You are my strength and my shield. You are my wall."

Later in the day, a guard came to me and gave me the news that my father-in-law had died. I was saddened, but I knew the Lord was with me.

Something greater than my death sentence was happening in my life. God was showing me how to pray and what would happen when I prayed.

A part of me began to question, "Could this all be a coincidence? Am I starting to lose my mind in prison?" I knew that there were stories of people who spent so much time in solitary confinement that they went insane. "However," I thought to myself, "even if I were going insane for God, what else would I do with my time?"

Even though I was a little skeptical, I started to see the future of little things—things that didn't seem so significant. One day in prayer, I saw a plate with apples and grapes. When I saw the vision, I was instantly hungry for the sweetness of apples and grapes. Fruits have sugar that I crave, and I hadn't had any fruit in so long.

After seeing the vision, I waited upon the Lord. I didn't feel the need to make it happen or to manipulate the future to fulfill the vision. I knew that either the vision was of God, or it wasn't. If God gave me the vision to foretell the coming of fruit, then it was not my place to ask the guards to bring me fruit. However, just to have a witness of the vision that God gave me, I decided to tell a guard about the vision, but I did it in a careful way.

"Mmm…you know what I could really go for today?" I said, nonchalantly. The guard did not answer or even look at me. She just ignored me. "I could really go for some fruit."

She laughed out loud, bending a bit at the waist as she thought of the ridiculousness of the idea of getting fresh fruit in prison. I know that she did not make a lot of money, so most likely the idea of her getting fresh fruit was also a silly idea.

"No. Really. I am dreaming about some apples and grapes. I would really love apples and grapes."

Prisoners often dream of food, so it didn't seem like anything out of the ordinary to discuss, so just for kicks and giggles, I decided to add some spice to it. "I think I will have some."

"Have some what?" the guard asked.

"Some grapes and apples. I think I will have some," I said with a mischievous smile.

"Oh, that will be the day," she said again with a laugh.

The very next day, the same guard came to my cell announcing I had a visitor. I rarely had visitors, as even my children had been kept from visiting me. She led me to the visitor center. When I entered in, I had a priest waiting for me. The priest had come to pray with me and to encourage me.

Before our time was over, he gave me a gift. It was a large plastic bag of apples and grapes!

When the guard returned to take me back to my cell, she saw the large bag I had of apples and grapes and was amazed. She remembered the words that I had spoken earlier and knew that there was no way of me knowing. I had no communication with the outside world and my visit had not been arranged previously. I didn't have a phone, access to email, friends to chat with, or even guards to slide me information.

It amazed me as much as it did her!

"I can't believe that yesterday you were telling me that you were going to get apples and grapes. How did you know?" she asked, losing all disciplined prison guard demeanor in her voice. In that moment of excitement, she became a person again and we were two normal women chatting together in amazement.

"I didn't know," I responded. "God just answered my prayer."

"So, you asked for apples and grapes and God gave them to you? Is that it?"

"Umm...kind of," I responded, not knowing if she would understand if I tried to explain that I didn't actually ask for them but agreed with God after seeing them. I wasn't fully understanding everything myself. How could I possibly explain it to her?

"Well, if God answers your prayers for apples and grapes, perhaps you should have prayed for your freedom."

We both laughed.

"I will be released," I responded. "I will be free."

She looked at me with a smile, but I grabbed my chest. "Did that just come out of my mouth?" I said silently as I stepped back into my prison cell on death row.

24

THE RESURRECTION OF DRY BONES

Out of the blackness of a hundred nights came an unmistakable glory shining forth that was so bright that I could see it even with my eyes shut. Darkness fled from Him, running and hiding. I knew it was Him because His glow warmed like a winter hearth. I didn't need to ask His name and He knew mine.

It was Jesus! His presence had the familiar silence that I had grown to trust. I had never seen Him face-to-face, but He was not a stranger.

"Lord," I said, starting the petitions of a daughter to a loving Father. "Heal my body."

He was silent. I felt too timid to speak again, but I mustered up the strength to squeeze out the next sentence.

"Lord, give me freedom."

Again, He was silent.

"Lord, please let me see my children."

Silence.

"Lord! Let me see my husband."

Silence.

"Lord!" I cried out with more angst than I had ever mustered in my bones, "Just let me die!" I was on my knees begging Him to show me at least enough mercy to let me die and end my misery. Allow my death to end my humiliation in front of my enemies.

He remained silent, but the absence of noise was not a lack of compassion, but the opposite. I was not anxious in His presence. My natural disposition was to do what I had done since my arrest and simply sink, but without a word He lifted me up. The same quiet hand of grace that reached down without saying a word to pull Peter out of the stormy waters was the same hand that reached down and rescued me.

It was impossible for me to doubt in His presence, in His hands. I was born and transformed into a little girl again. His grace was the answer to my salvation. He didn't need words. At that moment He taught me I didn't need words either.

I had always heard His answer to my questions, but never listened. Now I was listening. In the hush of an unspoken answer, I found peace. The Bread of Life ended my hunger. Without the noise of words, I was humbled at the cross and lay on the ground, prostrate at the feet of my loving Savior. He never left me. He never forsook me. He never abandoned me.

"I will listen, oh Lord, to the response of the cross. When I struggle to find strength through strife, I will tune my ear to the sound of the stone that has already rolled away. What You have done has already provided the answer of what You will do. What You have said answered my questions long before I had them. I will praise You for what You have already done, because it announces what You will do! I have lived all this time thinking that I must love You although You didn't answer my cries when I was in my darkest moment. Oh, the mercy You have shown for not hearing the answers that You have already given!

"When I demanded an answer, You catered to me with delicate, silent grace. Only silent grace can explain the lack of harsh correction."

"Forgive me, oh Lord, for not fully understanding that every answer can be found in the cross."

I had so many questions, but in the presence of Jesus they were all answered, and His answers changed my life—gave me life. I found salvation. I had already given my life to Christ as a young girl, but I felt reborn with a renewed mind. I no longer felt like I was facing death but was now living a new life with a new understanding of all things—not a complete understanding, but a new vantage point that made all things new.

"I am ready to come with You, Jesus," I said looking up and realizing that the world had nothing left for me.

"Not yet," He replied.

"Please, Jesus! Please let me come with You!" I cried. The closer I tried to get, the further I seemed to slip away. I strived to grab onto Him, but He was too far away. Suddenly, my eyes opened, and I was no longer beside Jesus but was back in my cell again. Pain shot through my chest.

"Help!" I cried out, feeling as if I were dying. "Help!" I said again a little louder, hoping the guard would hear me without having to force out the word again.

"I need a doctor! A doctor please!"

I had passed out, and I knew the problem. I was diabetic. My body was literally attacking itself and the situation was urgent.

"Shut up in there!" the guard yelled. "You don't need a doctor, but you might need one if you don't shut up."

"But I just passed out. I have diabetes, and the situation is a medical emergency."

"I am telling you if you do not shut up," the woman said while banging the bars with her worn wooden club, "I am going to give you a medical emergency. I will beat you so badly that they will have to carry you out of your cell on a stretcher."

"Dear Jesus!" I cried out, putting my hand on my chest to pray for myself. "I need Your healing. In Your holy name, I plead for Your healing power to touch Your servant's body and supernaturally restore my health." Within minutes, I felt a warm sensation go throughout my entire body.

As soon as I cried out to God, I heard His sweet voice soothe my soul with the same words He said to His disciples in Matthew chapter six, *"Can any one of you by worrying add a single hour to your life?"* (Matthew 6:27 NIV).

"No, Lord," I answered. "I can't add anything to my life by worrying, but I know that You and You alone have the power to heal."

Soon after my prayer, my spell passed, but another prisoner fainted and passed out. Their medical condition was also urgent, but since they were not being charged with blasphemy, the prison warden sent for a medical doctor to check on the situation.

With a doctor so close, the prison warden figured he might as well make the most of it and send the doctor to my cell as well. The doctor confirmed that my blood sugar level and my blood pressure were both elevated above normal and gave me medication to bring them back under control.

"Thank You, Jesus, for the healing," I prayed silently, noting both the doctor and the medicine that he gave me were a direct answer to prayer for Jesus to heal my body. I know that there are many people that would not agree with me and would argue that medicine is not an answer to prayer, but I believe that *all healing* is an answer to prayer. God brings healing to His children and sometimes He chooses to use His children in the process.

"Thank You, Jesus, for Your healing." I prayed again. I began to praise Jesus openly. I was already on death row, and I knew they planned to kill me. I was in solitary confinement. There was nothing more they could do to me. Even if they beat me, at least that would keep me company, and I wouldn't be alone so much.

"Why are you talking to yourself all the time?" the guard shouted. "You are crazy! You know that? You are certifiably insane. You keep talking to someone that is not there. They should have you tested."

I knew that I sounded crazy, but I was not alone. Jesus was with me in the cell. I was growing more and more convinced of it as the days went on.

I still missed my children, but God showed me that He was looking after them. He also gave me a burden for the other mothers in the prison whose children did not have anyone to look after them. Some of the mothers went to bed at night knowing their children were being abandoned and abused. Some of the children had been sold as slaves. Others experienced even worse fates.

The mothers endured suffering that was worse than their prison situation. The women suffered without their children and didn't have a purpose in their suffering. I was gifted with purpose in my suffering. It's not what I suffer, but what I was suffering for that made all the difference.

In Pakistan, suffering was a part of our life. We all suffered, but why did we suffer? If I gave my life to Islam, I would suffer. If I give my life to Christ, I must suffer, but with Christ I suffer for a purpose that is greater than my suffering and makes the suffering bearable.

My faith in Jesus did not remove the pain during the times of intense suffering. My prayers did not take me out of prison, but they took the prison out of me. I had been wishing for my circumstances to change, but Jesus appearing to me made me realize that I was the one that needed to change in my circumstances.

I was reminded of Ezekiel when he was brought out by the Spirit of the Lord and shown a valley full of dry bones and God commanded him, *"Prophesy upon these bones, and say unto them, O ye dry bones, hear the word of the LORD. Thus saith the Lord GOD unto these bones; Behold, I will cause breath to enter into you, and ye shall live: and I will lay sinews upon you, and will bring up flesh upon you, and cover you with skin"* (Ezekiel 37:4–6 KJV). Then the Lord moved, and there was a noise and a rattling sound among the dry bones as they came together, grew flesh, and started to live again.

I imagined that, like Ezekiel, God had placed me in the valley to show all the dry bones that I had left behind. In my life I had left a trail of dusty bones in the school, in my home, and with my family. There were dusty bones in the streets and the shops that I visited. I left a white chalky dust trail on the bus and in the prison, sprinkling the lifeless ashes of a dead Christian faith everywhere I went. The bones of defeat in the courtroom and the dry ashy bones handed to me by the accusers were the remnants that I shared with others.

Everyone who looked at me saw a death sentence. I was the blasphemer that would be hanged for my crime, and my name-less body would be added to the heap of other nameless bodies killed in the name of Islam, but God breathed life into my death sentence and gave it meaning. Flesh, tendons, and muscle fiber began to grow on the skeleton of my death sentence to give it meaning. The meaning brought purpose to my valley of suffering.

Jesus's resurrection power brought forth life in the valley of bones. A new stirring was taking place, and it felt like the beginning and not the end.

25

PERSECUTION MAFIA

"**W**hat does that mean?" I asked my brother Joseph.

"It means that you no longer have a lawyer."

"Do I need a lawyer? I mean…I am sentenced to die. What does a dead woman need with a lawyer?"

"Shagufta, you can appeal. Your case is ridiculous. There is no justice in this case and the government of Pakistan knows it. The courts know it. The Muslim leaders know it. That is why they want you to stay silent. They do not want the world to see how they really are. Your case sheds light on the real situation and exposes their lies about human rights and justice," Joseph pleaded with angst in his eyes.

I could hear the disappointment and defeat in his voice as he told me that the lawyers in my case would no longer represent me. They simply didn't see a need to once I was sentenced to death. In the beginning I felt so fortunate that there were so many charity organizations that had come to help us. They knew so many things that I was ignorant of. Joseph, my brother, worked closely with them and campaigned hard on my behalf, but no matter what he did, he felt that he was running into a wall of apathy.

"The lawyer didn't help," I said.

"I don't think they were ever meant to help," he replied.

"What do you mean?"

Joseph paused for a moment, looking into the air, searching for the right words to say. "How do I put this?" he said. "I have learned a lot about this whole process and the more I learn, the more nauseous I feel."

I looked back at him inquisitively, trying to understand where he was going.

"When the government cheats us or Muslims condemn us, there is a part of me that expects it, but when Christians cheat us, there is something about it that cuts deeper."

"Who cheated us?"

"There is an entire industry out there built around getting rich off people like you. They take your case, use you as their poster child for persecution, and raise money off your suffering. They don't care about you, and they don't care about me. They only care about getting rich."

Joseph repositioned himself and pivoted toward me. "Why do you think they didn't fight hard at the trial? Do you think it was because they are bad lawyers?"

"It was because the Muslim judge would not let them say anything."

"Yes, but they were too easily convinced. They made a better case for you in front of the cameras than they did in front of the judge. The truth is, Shagufta, they make more money off you if you remain in prison. If they win your case too quickly or too easily, their 'money train' prematurely comes to a screeching halt. If you stay in prison for blasphemy, then these lawyers and human rights organizations can go around and raise money campaigning your victimhood to Christians around the world. The more extreme your sentence, the stronger sympathy they can extract from potential donors, and the more money they are able to make. It's life and death for you, but it is a game for them."

I sat back and thought about the words that he was saying.

"This is why your children are not able to come and see you, Shagufta. If you want the honest truth—there it is, plain and simple. Our family is making too much money off keeping your children in their home. They are now a meal ticket. Christians around the world are donating to our family to provide care for your children."

"I am happy for that!" I rebutted. "I am thankful my children are being cared for."

"Yes, but they are being withheld from you so that you do not make any changes to their living situation. Our relatives are using your children as their own income generator."

My heart dropped. I knew that was the situation and had tried to drive those thoughts from my mind, but Joseph confirmed my intuition.

220 Under Threat of Death

"It is just a mess!" Joseph continued sulking. "Your situation is simply too dangerous for any real lawyer to touch and anyone too eager to help is basically looking to enrich themselves."

"Is it that bad?" I asked in disbelief.

"Yes! This is literally a Mafia ring of con men looking to make money from persecuted Christians."

His words reminded me of the dilemma with slavery in Pakistan.

Although slavery has been banned for centuries, it is alive and well in Pakistan. I remember when Shafqat was first injured, and we needed money for his medical procedure. There were many loan sharks that were ready to give money, but I had already been warned. Almost thirteen million children are in slavery in Pakistan today because of loans that parents could not pay back.[3]

In Pakistan, when families are unable to pay back a loan, their children are often given as payment. Many Christians around the world have witnessed this and have made attempts to help, not realizing their help often hurts. Many Christians, unknowingly, come to the aid of these child slaves and in the process, support the slave industry in Pakistan and help it increase.

When Christians are confronted with the child slave industry in Pakistan, their knee-jerk reaction is to help get these children out. Upon learning that the children were sold into slavery to pay a loan for their family, Christian organizations offer to pay off the loan to buy the freedom of the children. Without intending it to happen, this creates a market of supply and

---

3. Suhki, "Killed at Age 12 for Telling the World about 13M Child Slaves in Pakistan, Iqbal Masih," *Medium*, May 9, 2020, https://medium.com/social-jogi/killed-at-age-12-for-telling-the-world-about-13m-child-slaves-in-pakistan-iqbal-masih-b75c80848bbc.

demand. The more children that Christians "buy the freedom for," the higher the prices for child slaves go and the more lucrative the slave trade business becomes for slave owners.

Non-slave owners are enticed to invest and become new players in the slave market when they see how lucrative the slave industry has become due to western Christians that are willing to pay higher than market price for slaves.

On the other side, parents that get their children back are then able to freely obtain another loan again, using their child as collateral.

Sadly, Christians feel good about buying the freedom of small children that were forced into slavery, and do so in good faith, but have in fact supported the industry that perpetuates it. The same concept is true for the "persecution Mafia." Upon hearing the needs of persecuted believers in prison, Christians want to help, and they often do so by sending financial donations through foundations and charities that have been specifically set up to benefit from those funds.

We were new to this and were ignorant. The "persecution Mafia" benefits the most off poor, uneducated families like ours.

Soon after my case went public, Joseph connected with a bishop in Karachi to find a lawyer, who gave us advice to connect with a group that he knew had experience with cases similar to mine. Little did we know that they had very little incentive to get me out of prison, but benefited the most when I remained in. We quickly learned that they did not have an interest in getting me released, but instead desired to get as much media attention as possible—not in the Pakistani media, but in the foreign media.

They share the names of big lawyers with the foreign news outlets and create the illusion of a busy network working 24/7, putting pressure on politicians, judges, and influential individuals, but everything they do costs a lot of money.

Once they have the money from overseas Christian donors, nothing happens. The money is never for the victim, because it was never meant to be. It is a scam, and Christians are their targets.

In our case, the organization that campaigned for my case paid a lawyer to represent me, but they didn't appear in court, did not launch any significant defense strategy, and in the end, they too easily conceded defeat when I was given the death sentence.

Having never been exposed to this kind of corruption, Joseph had many arguments with the aid organization and the lawyer that were working with us. He could see that they were not doing anything to help and didn't understand why—until he understood that it was a financial scam—not a real defense effort. He had been fooled.

These types of charities do not actually want Christian persecution in Pakistan to go away, because if it did go away, they would lose their goose that lays the golden eggs. I was one such hen. According to my brother, hundreds of thousands of dollars were raised in my name to aid my situation, but those funds never made it past the pockets of the foundation directors.

"I am not worried, Joseph," I said, putting his mind at ease. "This is in God's hands."

I was reminded of the story of Shadrach, Meshach, and Abednego. (See Daniel 3.) Now that I was facing death, I could directly relate to the story. Just as I could have saved myself by simply bowing to the god of Islam, they too could have saved their lives by bowing to the king, but they refused. Their words to the king resonated with me when they said, "*Our God whom we serve is able to deliver us from the burning fiery furnace, and he will deliver us out of your hand, O king. **But if not**, be it known to you, O king, that we will not serve your gods or worship the golden image that you have set up*" (Daniel 3:17–18 ESV).

Those words surged into my blood and gave me courage and strength. After the vision of Jesus, I had a new comfort of knowing that He had the power to deliver me from the hands of the Pakistani government and save me from certain death if He wanted to, but if He chose not to, like Shadrach, Meshach, and Abednego, I would still not serve the god of Islam and would continue to serve only the King of kings all the way to death.

26

BONDING WITH ASIA

Without warning my cell began shaking, and the cracks that I had been admiring every day in the ceiling suddenly turned into A-shaped concrete fragments falling from the sky. They crashed on the ground below like flat, dry pieces of stale cake, and I covered my head and curled up into the fetal position, crying out to God for protection.

The entire prison started to sway, and screams of death rang out in the air. It felt apocalyptic. The actions of the evil prison guards flashed before their own eyes as their lives tipped back and forth in the balance. The dominant act of God revealed how fragile we all are, both guard and prisoner. Death is the great equalizer.

I was not afraid. I knew where I was going. I knew the Lord was with me and I would not die one second sooner than He would allow.

I thought of the story of Paul and Silas, when they were praying and singing around midnight and then, without warning, a great earthquake hit and destroyed their entire jail cell (see Acts 16:25–28). I heard a large cracking sound and looked over to see the entire back wall on the side of my cell collapse. Just as the jailhouse of Paul and Silas fell to the ground and allowed them to simply walk out, so too did mine. Just as Paul and Silas did not attempt to escape, I too stayed in the location where my cell used to be.

When the earth finally stopped shaking, there was a sound of relief that swept through the entire prison.

Just before the earthquake started, I had been praying, and the Lord showed me that there was going to be shaking that would hit the prison. He did it for Paul and Silas, and I knew that He would also do it for me. First it would happen in the natural and then it would happen in the spiritual. The earthquake hit, and not a hair on my head was injured. The Lord kept me protected through the entire situation. Although my small cell crumbled all around me and fell to the ground, not one single piece of concrete fell on me.

In the spiritual world, there was an earthquake about to shake the foundations. I learned that there were fellow believers in the prison together with me, including Asia Bibi.

I knew Asia Bibi's story from before I was arrested. She was also from Punjab and was charged with blasphemy like I was. I had never met her before, but I remember her story well, because Muslims all over the country were angry over it. Asia had simply taken a drink of water from a cup where Muslim women drank, making it unclean and angering them.

What really sparked the outrage among the Muslim leaders was that she didn't just endure the verbal attacks on her faith but defended her faith; that was the real reason she was sentenced to death.

Many of the actions of the prophet Muhammad are indefensible, so the only way to defend his actions is to make it illegal to say anything about them. Asia Bibi's case was an embarrassment to the entire nation of Pakistan, because it exposed the real situation of life under Islamic rule. There was no desire by the Muslim leaders to change the law, but instead, they just wanted to make it illegal to talk about the law. The quicker they could dispose of her, the better they would feel.

Asia's cell was not far from mine. I could not see her, but I could hear her voice. She was also in solitary confinement. Both of us were kept from each other and the general population for our own safety. There were so many people in the prison who would love to kill us for the honor of Islam.

There was an unconfirmed rumor that had circulated around the prison that Asia was going to be the first woman in Pakistan's history to be executed for blasphemy. If that was true, I would be the second, following right behind her. It was not the kind of thing that I wanted to be remembered for.

When we first met each other, we immediately had a connection. I had been waiting so long to find a friend, and now I had one! We were both mothers and were both put in prison for blasphemy. We were also both facing false accusations against us.

We found a kind of odd bond where we both lived in a land where the mere allegation of speaking words meant more than our lives. Our lives, mothers or not, were disposable, but the words we were accused of saying were not.

I would have done anything to be locked away in her cell. I had not had anyone to talk to for years. I am such a social creature and have always enjoyed being in the presence of others.

Before Asia, I had so much to say, but no one to say it to. I had so much love to give, but no one to share it with. I yearned for a normal conversation—any conversation. I didn't even need to talk. I would have settled to simply sit and listen to someone else talk. Just to have human contact of any kind would have reminded me that I was alive.

A simple letter from a family member, friend, or stranger would have made all the difference, but the letters never came. I would have been happy to read someone else's letter just to have something to read!

If I could have only seen a picture of my children, it would have brought nourishment to my soul, but it was not allowed.

Instead, I sat alone and told myself jokes, shared worthless compliments to empty spaces, and retold stories that I hadn't heard in a while. Now I had someone to talk to, even if I could not see her.

Our cells were roughly five meters apart, and the guards walked back and forth between our two cells to make sure we didn't try to communicate. If I got extra food, I would hang on to it and when there were no guards around, I would throw it over to her cell. After I got good at it, I tossed other things as well.

I felt giddy, just knowing that she was over there receiving things that I had saved for her. I had always loved to give gifts, and this was an outlet for me to express my love language.

Sometimes I would hear her also throw things my way, like extra fruit, bread, or nuts. It was nice to know that she was also thinking of me when she had extra food in her cell. We were looking out for each other.

If we were ever allowed out of our cell, it was never at the same time. The prison wanted to make sure that they kept us completely separated.

There were times that we would encourage one another with songs. A special Christian song would occasionally come to my mind, and I would belt it out, knowing that it would bring encouragement to her soul. Neither of us were great singers, but it didn't matter. I would sit in my cell with my back to the wall and sing a melody of praise to the Father, sway back and forth with my eyes closed, knowing that He could hear it. When her voice would softly join in from a distance, it was like a healing salve to my soul.

One day without even noticing it, I began to hum a tune of a special Punjabi Christian praise and worship song. "Jehovah, I am calling upon You to come toward me. Jehovah, I am calling on You to come listen to me. Jehovah, I am calling on You to come protect me. God, see my trouble and give me freedom."

I had completely forgotten that Asia could hear me. After only a few minutes however, in the distance, I could hear the faint sound of her humming along with me. I sang out the words of the song and she sang along, word for word.

"Jehovah, I am calling upon You to come toward me. Jehovah, I am calling on You to come listen to me. Jehovah, I am calling on You to come protect me. God, see my trouble and give me freedom," I sang aloud. This was a popular Urdu praise and worship song.

"Sing with me, Asia!" I said, encouraging her to sing the words louder.

"Your voice is so beautiful," she replied. "You sing it. I want to listen."

I sang it in Urdu, and I sang it out loud.

The only time that we were ever able to see each other was during special holidays. Every Christmas and Easter, we would put in a request to pray together. We were given forty minutes to come together to pray during those special holidays.

We were not allowed to pray alone, however. The prison wanted us to be monitored the entire time. Guards were stationed to stand beside us and listen to our prayers. It felt awkward to pray beside them. In the beginning, I was afraid that I would say something wrong or offend them and get into even more trouble with the prison guards, but then I asked myself, "What more can they do to us? Both Asia and I have been given the death sentence, and we are both in solitary confinement."

I couldn't see my husband, my children had been taken away, I had no friends or freedom, and I would soon be hanged. I had nothing left to fear, and I was certain that Asia felt the same.

With nothing to fear, we prayed for whatever we wanted to pray for. We prayed for each other and our families, but then we also prayed for the guards. We prayed for their safety, their families, and their salvation.

They were uncomfortable with us praying for them, but they couldn't stop us. The more we prayed, the more uncomfortable they grew. I sensed they wanted us to stop, but it emboldened me somehow. I didn't mean to hurt them or make them feel uncomfortable, but I was no longer afraid.

The guards were not only compelled to listen to us, but they had to take notes and write down everything they heard us say. As I held Asia Bibi's hands, our spirits joined together as one. The focus of our prayers also aligned as one. It was a connection that I was thirsty for.

I could see the same in Asia and hear it in her voice when she prayed. She was no longer worried about her own situation, and she let loose a flood of love for those who were persecuting us.

We didn't only pray for prison guards, but for the prison leaders and administration as well. We prayed for their families to be blessed and for them to know the love of Christ.

As we prayed, the guards were quickly scribbling notes of our words. It filled my heart with joy that they had to write down the testimony of the love of Christ and share it with others who would also be forced to read it. We were sharing the Gospel with the unreached!

Asia and I prayed for our fellow prisoners and for the government to have mercy upon them. We prayed for their children. As mothers, we both knew the heart and pain that a mother suffers when they are away from their children.

We prayed that God would show favor on the prisoners and that the government would grant them an early release to go and be with their families. In the beginning it seemed we could not be completely intimate with God because of the lack of privacy, but in that moment, we had the most intimate time with Him—giving Him praise during the storm.

A new Christian guard in the prison brought a Bible for me and slipped it between the bars. Neither Asia or I were educated enough to read well, but I had grown accustomed to looking at the words in the Bible and trying to understand the sounds. Over time I had gotten better.

From the little schooling I had as a little girl, I could remember the words of my teacher and make out some of the sounds, and over time I started to recognize the patterns. There were times where I could guess one word and I would remember the story and know what story I was looking at.

We couldn't really read every single word in the Bible, but there was a comfort in praying together and having God's Word with us.

The time that Asia and I spent singing praise songs, lifting the name of the Lord up in prayer, and seeing each other during Christian holidays were invaluable. Her voice brought daily comfort and encouragement to me, and seeing her face-to-face was an overwhelming joy.

After about three years, Asia's charges were overturned. Her legal fight was deadly, resulting in several bloody protests around the country and the assassination of two high officials.

Her release from prison gave me immediate hope. After she was released, she brought my name up in several interviews and in talks with leaders around the world.

She did not forget me.

27

REFUSAL TO DENY

The relentless sun bounced off my lonely cell repeatedly with rays that retreated, rolled back into the ocean waves of incandescence, and returned to do it again. I was slowly cooking in an oven of clay-baked solitude, finding the motionless misery absent of speech or sound. There wasn't any ventilation or circulation in my cell. Only the light buzzing sound of the sun's rays could be heard dancing in my head an octave higher than my ear was accustomed to. If you hold your ear close to a toaster, you can hear the same humming sound of heat as my cell.

My days were long, anguishing, and windless. I had nothing to take my mind off the heat—nothing to distract me. The stale heat quietly hovered over pools of my evaporated tears marked only with white traces of salt. I couldn't find relief. "This is what hell must feel like," I thought to myself at least a thousand times a day. The heat of Pakistan's flames was just as hot and as inextinguishable as Hades.

I could hear the words, *"Send Lazarus that he may dip the tip of his finger in water and cool my tongue; for I am tormented in this flame"* (Luke 16:24 NKJV), as the rich man pleaded Abraham in the book of Luke. I knew the words all too well. They were seared in my soul with a hot iron, because I too was a beggar of relief. The evil banners of heat flapped and furled up against my mustard seed of faith.

"Take me into Your loving arms, Father. I wish only to wear a crown of solace. Send forth a hush that quiets the gnashing of teeth. Only You can set me free. Only Your love can give me freedom."

Other women on death row were allowed to have an air cooler in their cell, but I was not. The air coolers were not fancy, only a fan blowing a breeze over a jug of water, often called a swamp cooler, but they provided enough relief for sleep.

Several times I was told that if I converted to Islam, my death sentence would be turned into life in prison. I always said no, and this heat reminded me why. A life sentence of being locked away in a solitary box, without my husband, without my children—confined to this small space in extreme heat was not something that I could do forever. In Pakistan, life in prison is not mercy; it is a slow, torturous death allowing you the unique ability to watch yourself die one degree at a time.

Muslims were constantly offering me mercy, the mercy of Allah that would allow me to deny my identity as a follower of Jesus Christ, the mercy to live life in the oppressive submission extended to women, the mercy of slowly roasting in the tortuous heat of a prison cell, the mercy of living life without love.

Muslims threatened to kill me and save my life at the same time and scoffed at me when I failed to see how their offer to rescue me from the danger that only they posed was not merciful. They forced me to drink a poison and considered it mercy by offering the antidote. I wouldn't survive much more of their abundant mercies.

I was not kicked or punched while in prison, but the mercy of hate tortured me every day. I was despised and thought of as an enemy of the people. Out of mercy, I was sentenced to hanging.

If I didn't die from the noose for blasphemy, then I would die from an abundance of Islam's mercy.

The truth is, I wasn't meant to be comfortable. The prison was designed in a way that I would not find any comfort in my purposefully hot, cramped cell, but God was telling me that my time in prison was limited. When the earthquake hit, many things changed. My cell crumbled around me, and God was showing me that the same was taking place in the legal system as well. I stopped relying on man to help me get out and left my fate in the hands of God.

The prisoners and guards were all amazed at how my cell collapsed, but I was not injured. Though they mocked me in the day, in private, many were seeking me out and requesting that I pray for them. Rumors started to spread around the prison that I could see the future and pray for healing. Women who used to openly ridicule me were now secretly sending me prayer requests begging for healing. Women who were in prison for murder, drugs, and prostitution looked for prayer for their children and families. They requested prayer for their marriages to be restored.

God spoke to me and showed me how to minister in the lives of these women that had been abandoned by society and forgotten by the world. One by one, prayers were answered, addictions were broken, peace came to families, and diseases were healed.

Even Arshad was changing. Arshad was a massive presence of a woman who worked as a guard. Her large muscular shoulders always hunched forward as she gazed down into my cell and snarled her commands at me day after day. She was as cruel as she was abusive and enjoyed watching me suffer. In her mid-forties, Arshad had a callous attitude that had been layered with scar tissue over the years.

Though it was clear from her scarf that she was a female, there were not many indicators that she was a human, let alone a woman. She walked with her legs widened and took heavy thudding steps like a man and growled under her breath like a beast. When I thought of the guards that I was the most afraid of in all of Multan Prison, it was Arshad who filled my nightmares with terror, but things had started to change.

I no longer feared her, and she could sense it. I didn't announce it. I didn't tell her I wasn't afraid of her. I don't even know when I became aware of it myself, but something had changed. God gave me hope and His hope wiped away all fear in my life.

I hadn't realized it before, but fear made me useless for the kingdom. It wasn't until I was filled with the hope of Christ that I could rightly express the love of Christ. In my fear, I clung to the love of Christ for self-preservation. Fear is selfish, but hope is generous.

"Please pray for me," came the desperate pleas of a young Muslim woman brave enough to venture close to my cell. "I have been sent here away from my children and need to find a way to be closer. My family is too poor to drive them to this prison every day."

I told her that I would pray for her in the name of Jesus. I prayed aloud and didn't flinch at the judging stares of the guards. The entire prison was full of conversations when only a few days later the woman was given her orders to transfer prisons. The prison that she was sent to was closer to her family and children, just as she had asked.

"You are such a gift from God in this dark prison," she told me just before she left.

"Prayers can break the chains of slavery," I told her before she walked away. I wanted her to know that it wasn't me, but it was God who had answered her prayers. He is a living God and actively hears the prayers of His children. He is not a passive listener. "If you continue to pray, God will move the mountains. You need to remember that the solution to your problem is prayer."

Psalm 121 says, "*I will lift up mine eyes unto the hills, from whence cometh my help*" (Psalm 121:1 KJV). I look not at the mountains but beyond the mountains where the answer to my prayers resides. It is easy to look at the mountains of challenges towering over us in our lives and pray for salvation, but the mountains are not the focus. It is the help that is coming beyond the mountains that brings hope.

I began quoting Psalm 91 to myself before going to sleep, *"Whoever dwells in the shelter of the Most High will rest in the shadow of the Almighty. I will say of the LORD, 'He is my refuge and my fortress, my God, in whom I trust'"* (Psalm 91:1–2 NIV). This psalm brought so much hope to my life, especially when I got to the part that says, *"You will not fear the terror of night, nor the arrow that flies by day, nor the pestilence that stalks in the darkness, nor the plague that destroys at midday.... With long life I will satisfy him and show him my salvation"* (verses 5–6, 16 NIV).

The hope of the Lord was not only changing my life, but it was impacting the prison around me. The lives of the prisoners were being transformed. In the eyes of the prison, I was a Christian—which made me an enemy of Islam and by default, made me an enemy of Pakistan, but I was no longer afraid.

There were many people in Pakistan who were saddened at the delay of my execution, but they were at least placated a little bit at the idea of my suffering. Now they didn't even have that to cling to.

There was a gleeful reassurance for conservative Muslims if they believed I suffered every minute of every day before my death. Pakistani people who didn't have a natural inclination to hate me were persuaded to hate me because of the bad press I brought to the nation of Pakistan, but now my suffering was being robbed from them.

My death sentence was now a plague on the nation of Pakistan. It was causing the entire nation to suffer. The international news media reported on the persecution of vulnerable women by Pakistan's blasphemy laws in Europe, the United

States, Australia, Singapore, Japan, and other nations. The Pakistani people knew that their Islamic laws looked backwards and barbaric to the rest of the world when shared openly in the news. It was impossible for world leaders to take the Pakistani delegation seriously when they had laws that killed mothers for supposedly sending unflattering texts. Every day they kept me in prison brought hardship upon them.

The media in Spain started to report on my situation, giving Joseph an opportunity to meet with the top cardinal to get the pope involved. My words spoken to the guards when they proposed that I convert to Islam had made their way all the way to the Vatican. "Jesus Christ sacrificed His life for me though I am a sinner. I will never, ever change my religion and convert to Islam. I would rather be hanged than deny Jesus Christ."

The government of Spain offered my family and I political asylum if Pakistan would agree to let me go. My brother had taken custody of my children to look after them on my behalf. The Spanish government even gave Joseph a special residence card for travel and for his residency in Spain while he continued working on my case.

My refusal to deny Christ was being heard in the European Parliament and Pakistan's image was being tarnished more and more by the day. The international community was able to see that blasphemy cases like mine were not just a fluke or rare situation. Women and innocent believers persecuted under the law of persecution were a regular occurrence.

I grew bolder by the day, praying, "Risen Lord and Savior Jesus Christ, You sacrificed Your life for me though I am a sinner. I will never, ever change my religion. I will never convert to Islam. I would rather be hanged than deny You, but I can't stay in this prison any longer. My mind is going mad. I am losing all control of my senses."

28

THE MIRACULOUS CHANGING TIDES

The LORD is my shepherd, I lack nothing. He makes me lie down in green pastures, he leads me beside quiet waters, he refreshes my soul. He guides me along the right paths for his name's sake. Even though I walk through the darkest valley, I will fear no evil, for you are with me; your rod and your staff, they comfort me. (Psalm 23:1–4 NIV)

I clung to the words of Psalm 23, reminding me that the Lord is my Shepherd even on death row. I didn't need to be a smart lamb, a strong lamb, or a clever lamb—I just needed the Lord as my Shepherd. He provided for me, a silent lamb living among the wolves that desired to devour me. I didn't need to fear. My Shepherd leads me to green pastures of safety and peace. His rod and staff are not for fear, but comfort. He does not use his rod to beat His sheep; He uses it to protect them from the enemy.

I felt the tides shifting. I could not put my finger on anything or point to any significant event, but my spirit was changing. The Lord was giving me dreams and visions that were all pointing to a door opening to freedom. I knew that the dark forces of hell were against me, but I could not feel them because the rod of my Shepherd was protecting me. He had led me beside still waters and I didn't need to fear the enemy's attack.

I had no reason to feel more hopeful. All the signs were pointing to reasons why I should not have any hope at all. I should have been in a state of despair. I didn't have a lawyer defending me or making an appeal on my behalf. My entire legal team had abandoned me, but I felt good about it. I felt safer without the lawyers that had been representing me. They seemed like ambulance chasers to me, trying to use me and my family to benefit their pockets. I wasn't demoralized because they were gone, but instead I rejoiced that God had rid me of them.

Even if I did have a lawyer, I didn't have a way to pay them. The Christian organizations that had backed me in the past were no longer beside me and were no longer raising money to help us with our legal bills. Strangely, my legal situation was the same now that I didn't have a lawyer as when I did, and not having a lawyer was free!

After my initial arrest, there were lawyers and fundraisers clamoring on my behalf, but the closer I got to my execution, the fewer fundraising efforts were held for my benefit. My situation was not as lucrative for fundraising efforts as before. The funds dried up, and all I had left to depend on was God. I was content with that. I was in a better place after the money dried up and the lawyers fell by the wayside.

I found myself talking to God a lot more than I ever had. He was no longer a spiritual being somewhere in the sky, but He was personal to me. He was no longer this heavenly Father far away, but was a close friend, walking with me and bringing comfort to my life. I saw impossible miracles happen in the prison and knew that there was nothing that He could not do. I saw Him move in the lives of others and knew that He could also move in my life as well.

I knew that if He wanted me out of prison, I would be out, but "not my will, but His be done" (see Luke 22:42).

Outside the prison, the Lord was moving in miraculous ways. I hadn't seen my husband or children in years, but I knew that something was changing. I hadn't heard from my brother Joseph in weeks, but I knew that something was happening. I didn't know what would happen or when, but God was putting a spirit of expectation within me, telling me that a shaking was coming that would rock the foundations of the prison like the earthquake.

"Shagufta!" I heard the guard yell from down the hall, breaking my thoughts. I sat up in my cot and looked toward the door of my cell. "Shagufta!" came the bark again, accompanied by the jangling of keys. "Get up! You have a visitor!"

"A visitor?" I silently said to myself. Every time I heard that announcement, I wondered if it would be the day that I would finally get to see my children again. My heart was constantly dreaming images of my little Zain, Danish, Sheroz, and Sara. I imagined how they must have grown over the years that I had been imprisoned. I knew the chances of seeing them were next to nothing, but anytime I had an unannounced visitor to the prison, I would silently hope that I would see their faces in the visiting room.

As the guard escorted me into the visitor area, I didn't see anyone I recognized. The guard stopped, pivoted to the side and used her arms to introduce me to a man staring directly at me with a large caring smile on his face.

"Hello, Shagufta. My name is Saif ul-Malook. I am a lawyer, and I am here at the request of your brother Joseph to review your case."

The way he spoke instantly brought comfort to my soul and I knew that he was an answer to prayer. He was not a Christian, but I was certain that God had ordained him to be there with me on that day.

"Shagufta," he said in a very slow calming voice, while taking a seat at the visitors table, "there are many things to discuss about your case." I sat down in a seat across from him while studying his face.

Saif ul-Malook did not look or act like any of the lawyers that I had in the past. He didn't seem nervous or anxious, but instead had a very grandfatherly presence that took command of a room with soft wisdom. His tanned face, defined with deep crevices that dropped from his smiling cheeks down to his orb-shaped chin, was highlighted with his large silver-rimmed glasses.

"You know my brother Joseph?" I asked.

"I do, and I was also the lawyer for a good friend of yours that you might remember—Asia Bibi."

My heart immediately soared with just the mentioning of her name! "You were Asia Bibi's lawyer?" I screamed. "You must tell me, how is she doing? Where is she living?"

"Asia is doing well. She is living in Canada. She had to flee the country after she was released. I also had to leave the country last year after she was acquitted because of all the death threats against me and my family. I had to go to the Netherlands for a time until things calmed down. Now I have returned to take your case, because I believe that you have been wrongfully accused and should be released immediately."

"You think I am innocent?" I asked, wanting to hear the words again. I had spent every single day of the last seven years in prison hearing guards and fellow inmates calling me a blasphemer that I had forgotten that I had not actually committed the crime that I was accused of.

"I do think that you are innocent. The evidence against you is deeply flawed, to say the least, and the fact that you have been convicted based on it is a travesty."

"Look," Saif said, slowly shuffling his hands down by his waist to help him as he spoke. "I successfully pleaded Asia Bibi's case before the Supreme Court and was able to obtain her freedom because the evidence against her was preposterous and a gross miscarriage of justice. The evidence against you is even weaker!"

"But every lawyer that I have had argued against the evidence and lost. What makes this time different?" I asked.

"I don't know what your other lawyers presented to you or how you mounted your defense with them, but this case has no merit. Zero. There is no way the evidence against you can hold up in court. It simply can't."

"But they have a text that they say I sent to a local imam? Isn't that all the evidence they need?" I challenged.

"Do they?" he quipped back. "Do they actually have a text from you or your husband? Didn't they force your husband to sign a confession for a crime that they are also charging you with? Two death sentences for a text from a single phone? Shagufta, I looked at your case and it has no legs. It falls apart after the smallest questioning. I've studied your case and looked at all the documents. There is no proof that you ever sent those messages. The phone has never been proven to be in your possession."

I sat stunned as if I had just had the wind sucked out of me. He made it all sound so simple. "It is more complicated than that," I replied. "They said that I can't prove that I didn't have the phone that sent the text."

"No. It really isn't complicated. The burden of proof is on them to prove that you sent the text, not for you to prove you didn't. I studied your case and see that on July 20, 2013, a man by the name of Mohammad Hussain submitted a complaint at the Gojra police station in Toba Tek Singh district, Punjab. Right?"

I nodded. That sounded like what the other lawyers had shared with me.

"He alleged that he was praying at the mosque when he received a text message containing blasphemous text messages from a phone number that he didn't recognize. Mr. Hussain told the police that he personally went to a mobile franchise owner to figure out the identity of the owner of the phone from which the 'objectionable' message was sent. The franchise owner told him that he sold the SIM card to your husband. That is when they arrested you."

"But when they arrested us, they were shouting my name. They were looking for me, not my husband."

"Exactly!" Saif shot back. "The franchise owner switched his story under oath. He told the police your husband bought the SIM card. Then he reported you both bought it together. Then in front of the court he changed his statement, saying you bought the card while your husband waited outside. He testified that the number was registered under your name while your husband Shafqat footed the bill."

"Why did he change his statement?"

"He changed his statement for the same reason the judge sentenced you to death. He was afraid. The judge was afraid. Even your lawyers were afraid. The entire case against you isn't based on facts or evidence—they have no evidence. It is all based on fear!"

Fear! I thought to myself. We had all been caught in a cycle of the enemy's game of fear. I was afraid for my life, but God released me from that state of fear. I no longer had to be afraid. Saif's words were making me giddy.

I didn't want to get too excited. I was in front of a lawyer, not a judge. Saif ul-Malook was not a miracle worker. He didn't have the power to give me an acquittal, but he had taken the first step and shown that he was not going to live his life according to fear. His life had been threatened, and he was risking a lot by taking my case.

"You cannot survive here for much longer," he said, looking at me with compassion in his eyes.

"Why are you doing this?" I asked. I knew it wasn't because of the money because no amount of money is worth risking your life over. I knew it wasn't because I was a Christian, because he was a Muslim.

Without blinking, he looked back at me with conviction in his eyes and said, "When you defend someone accused of blasphemy, you are considered a blasphemer yourself. However, I am only doing my duty under the constitution and the law, which states that every accused person has the right to have his or her rights respected and to a fair trial. You deserve to have your right to a fair trial protected."

"So, what is the next step?" I asked eagerly.

"I personally do not see any reason why you should have to stay here. I firmly believe you will be acquitted, you will be released, and you will be with your children again and the good thing is that you are not alone."

I silently started to sob. I had never heard anyone speak about my case with so much faith. It was almost like he was prophesying. "I am not alone," I quietly sobbed.

Noticing my reaction, he repeated, "You are not alone. Your brother has been working with several great organizations like," he counted on his fingers, "the Jubilee Campaign, Alliance Defending Freedom International, and the European Union."

"The European Union?" I asked, completely shocked.

"Yes, there are several members of the European Parliament who have seen your case and are getting involved. Peter van Dalen, a Dutch member of the European Parliament picked up the case and brought it to the European Union. He wrote a resolution[4] to petition your case to the Pakistani government and in one day got sixteen thousand people to sign it!"

"Wow! Sixteen thousand people signed a petition for me?" I asked in shock. I really thought that I had been forgotten by everyone in the world, and somehow there were thousands of people out there thinking of me and petitioning for my freedom. I closed my eyes and started to thank God for all that He had done. He was moving even when I didn't know it. Even when I thought that I had been abandoned, He was there all along.

"Oh, he wasn't alone! Another member of the European Parliament, Charlie Weimers from Sweden, co-authored a resolution questioning whether the EU should continue allowing Pakistan to hold a major trade agreement because of the way that they have treated you. Weimers stood in front of the EU Parliament and passionately shared your case. He took it one step further by saying, 'Should Europe reward Pakistan's mob justice targeting Christians and its Prime Minister relativizing the Holocaust? My answer is no!'[5]

"Your case has no validity and people know it, Shagufta. The EU resolution to immediately review trade relations with Pakistan over your case passed overwhelmingly 662 to 3!"

"How did our government respond," I asked, half afraid to know the answer.

"Human Rights Minister Shireen Mazari immediately admitted, 'We have issues to resolve,' but almost begged there

4. Resolution on the blasphemy laws in Pakistan, in particular the case of Shagufta Kausar and Shafqat Emmanuel, 2021/2647(RSP), https://www.europarl.europa.eu/doceo/document/TA-9-2021-0157_EN.html.
5. Aizbah Khan, "PM Imran's 'Relativizing Holocaust' Irks Europe Approved Resolution Against Pakistan," BOL News, May 1, 2021, https://www.bolnews.com/international/2021/05/pm-imrans-relativizing-holocaust-irks-europe-approved-resolution-against-pakistan/?amp.

not to be any 'public positioning.' They want to talk about this in private. They want your case to be hidden. They do not want to openly discuss it, because it cannot be defended.

"Your case has been hidden for too long," he continued. "It is time that we shine some light on your case and show the world what you have been going through."

29

MEETING THE DELEGATION OF LIFE OR DEATH

As I sat in my cell, I found myself reciting Psalm 126 repeatedly. The last two verses replayed in my heart, *"Those who sow with tears will reap with songs of joy. Those who go out weeping, carrying seed to sow, will return with songs of joy, carrying sheaves with them"* (Psalm 126:5–6 NIV).

Psalm 126 was perfect for meditating on the goodness of Christ while I sat on death row. It's a lyrical reminder of God's people experiencing a time of weeping and sorrow but being able to draw strength from moments in the past filled with great joy and hoping for it again in the future.

Like the author of Psalm 126, my life was not as great as it once was. I believed that God was doing something in the midst of my trouble to make the days in the future even more joyful than they were in the past. Psalm 126 was my road map of hope.

It showed me where I was, where I came from, and where I was going. It helped me to suppress the voices of the demons that whispered to me every day that I was never going to get out of prison, never going to see my husband again, and never going to see my children again.

"I choose joy and not fear," I said to myself. "I choose joy and not fear."

"What are you saying?" a female guard demanded from a distance.

"Nothing," I immediately responded, not knowing anyone was listening. "I didn't know anyone was there."

"Well, lock it up in there. We have a delegation walking through the prison today."

Delegations came through every now and then to see the only women's prison in Punjab. Officials were often compelled to show the outside world how the conditions were for women in prison. These were usually good days because the guards would have to be extra nice to us to not raise any alarms with the delegation while they were there. I had no interest in talking to any visitors about my treatment in the prison, because I knew that once they left, I would be at the complete mercy of the guards. I didn't have any desire to make life more difficult for myself and didn't anticipate talking to anyone.

Not talking to visiting delegations was not difficult as the warden never brought official visitors to my section of the prison; however, after sitting on my cot for a few hours in the morning, I heard voices coming down the corridor. I could immediately tell that the voices were not prisoners or guards. Prisoners and guards have a completely different way of talking. I couldn't hear the subject of what they were discussing, but I could tell who was discussing it.

Prisoners talked in whispers when they roamed around the prison. Their hushed whispers were sometimes interspersed with moments of high-pitched giggles and laughs, which was completely different than a conversation between the guards. The voices of the guards were always purposeful, short and choppy when they conversed on their daily strolls. I would never hear a laugh from the guards unless it was a direct maniacal one, given only in sarcasm.

The voices that came down the corridor were more of a gentle humming sound. There was a tinge of kindness to them that was rarely, if ever, heard in the prison. As they got closer, I could tell they were not just regular visitors, but were city and provincial officials surrounded by an entourage. From the sound of their footsteps slapping against the hard concrete floor, I could tell they were getting closer, and it sounded deliberate.

One man who walked ahead of the others came up to my cell, looked at me, and then turned to those following and asked, "Is this her?"

"Yes, sir," echoed the familiar voice of one of the prison guards from the back. "That is prisoner Shagufta Kauser."

With that, the conversations among those following stopped and they all silently and curiously crowded around the outside of my cell, each shuffling around the others, trying to get a look inside.

"So, you are Shagufta," the bearded man in the western black suit said, peering in at me. He looked down and used both of his hands to flatten his tie. I looked back and simply nodded my head.

A guard in the back coughed a loud, fake cough indicating that I needed to stand and show respect to the delegation. Nervously, I slowly stood up. "Was this the visit before my execution tomorrow?" I thought to myself. "Did they all come to see the blasphemer before I die?"

Asia Bibi would have been the first female blasphemer to be executed in Pakistan under the new law, but since she was released, that left me next in line. It was a historical event. Everything seemed clearer now. I was about to make history.

No one said another word. There was a long awkward silence. They all looked at me, as I stood motionless in my cell. The cruelty of their stares forced my reflexes to engage them on equal ground. They were spectators, and I was their entertainment. Like a kicked dog in the corner, I simply wanted to curl up and die.

With a dizzying slow breath, I swallowed a slight taste of stomach acid and exhaled. I couldn't look up. I closed my eyes and tilted my head toward the ground. I wasn't afraid, but I refused to give the murderous league of government officials the expression they were looking for when they announced that I would be hanged soon.

I didn't hate them. To hate them was to become them. I only meant to keep them from seeing my face when they told me the news.

"We have something to tell you, Shagufta," the man said, breaking the silence.

I clenched my fists, stabilized my knees, and braced for it. My thoughts had no direction. They were in freefall.

"Your lawyer, Mr. uh…"

"Mr. Saif ul-Malook," said a woman behind him taking notes.

"Yes, your lawyer, Mr. Saif ul-Malook has made an appeal on your behalf to the Lahore High Court. The hearing for the appeal was scheduled for the third of June, but that was canceled."

I knew that Saif was making an appeal on my behalf, but I had not heard anything. I knew what no news meant. If it was good news, he would be the one sharing the details with me now.

"He appealed your case for three days before the court," he continued, but then stopped. "Shagufta," he said, "look at me. I have something to tell you."

I didn't want to open my eyes. I knew they would betray me if I had them open when they told me that I would be executed.

"Shagufta. You have been acquitted!" he said. "You are free to leave prison. Your death sentence has been overturned and you will be with your family again soon."

"What?" I said, bursting out in a scream. "How? What? Why? How?" I couldn't even think of what I was saying. It was all too much.

"There were more developments in your case in the last year than all the previous seven years combined. You have really been quite the problem for all of us. None of the courts wanted to hear your case, but when the high court in Lahore listened to your lawyer, it seemed that there was no real evidence against you. Your case was a hot potato! Your accusers changed their stories and didn't want to touch it. The phone that sent the text was never found. Your case was sent for appeal to Lahore High Court Chief Justice Mohammad Qasim Khan, then tossed to another senior judge from Rawalpindi, then to Lahore High Justice Shahbaz Ali Rizvi, then back to Rawalpindi, after that to the bench of Justice Tariq Saleem Sheikh and to Justice Muhammad Anwar-ul-Haq. The judges simply could not find any evidence against you."

"But they had a receipt?" I said foolishly, realizing I was making a case against myself all over again.

"Oddly, when your lawyer asked for that receipt so it could be reviewed, it was never produced. It seems there never was a receipt! It was made up!"

I laughed and cried at the same time. It was so absurd. I had been in prison for eight long years, and no one had even bothered to check the receipt that supposedly proved that I purchased a phone! I was sentenced to hang based on a false accusation and a fake receipt.

I fell to my knees laughing and crying. "Thank You, Jesus," I said out loud. No one tried to stop me. The guards didn't utter a word. I held my stomach and rocked back and forth on my knees. With tears rolling down my face, I wailed out again, "Thank You, Jesus!"

"It is very important that you do not tell anyone about your release," the man said. When I didn't respond, another man repeated what he had just said.

"Shagufta, I know that you are elated, but you must pay attention. Do not tell anyone about your release. You must keep it a secret. If others learn about the acquittal, your life and the lives of others in this correction facility will be in danger. Do you understand?"

I heard him and nodded my head, but I couldn't respond. I could barely breathe. All I could do was give praise to Christ. I was going home.

30

THE JOY OF FREEDOM

Security was increased throughout the entire prison with extra prison staff and more guards on duty. Even though I had been declared innocent by the courts, it didn't matter. There were still people who wanted to kill me. I was not innocent in the eyes of Islam. I was not innocent to Muslims. Whether I was guilty of blasphemy or not didn't matter, because I was guilty of being a Christian. I was guilty of rejecting Islam. That was all the real guilt needed and enough to make many Muslim leaders wish me dead.

Over a month had elapsed since the special delegation informed me about my acquittal. I was still locked up in my tiny cell and not allowed to leave. No one told me when I would be released or why I was still being held in prison. I didn't understand why I was still being held in prison if I had been found innocent and acquitted of all charges. The process of getting out of prison was a much slower moving one than the one that put me in prison. For Christians in Pakistan, it is quick and easy to be guilty, but slow and difficult to be proven innocent.

The last six weeks in prison felt like they lasted longer than the last seven years. The summer heat blasted my cell every day and cooked me relentlessly. The temperatures outside were over forty degrees Celsius and several degrees hotter in my cell. In the delirium of the heat, the enemy would whisper in my ear that I was never leaving Multan Prison alive, and the acquittal was all a dream, but when those moments came, I leaned on the vision I had of Jesus beside me. I knew that He was holding the prison door open, and I would be released.

Then one day a large military detail arrived at the prison early in the morning. Before lunch, the entire prison was surrounded by military trucks and personnel. There was more activity at the prison than usual with prison guards rushing back and forth, yelling for one another with a kind of urgency that was highly unusual.

After dinner that evening, one of the guards accompanying one of the top administrators of the prison came to my cell. "Shagufta, your son is here. Would you like to see him?" The words didn't seem real. I had been waiting to be released for several weeks but didn't think I would be able to see my children until after my release. I almost fainted. I had not seen any of my children for over seven years.

"My son is here?" I asked, barely able to finish the question before my voice cracked from crying. Looking back at the guard, I put my hand over my mouth, and nodded yes. "Yes, I would like to see him."

"He is waiting for you outside. You are being released this evening. We have a military escort ready to accompany you for your safety. Do you feel safe leaving together with your son?" The way the question was articulated didn't make sense to me, but I nodded yes anyway. I didn't want to risk anything that would prevent me from seeing my son.

I waited for a moment before catching my breath enough to answer the question. "Yes," I said, verbalizing a clear answer to accompany my head nod, so that there was no mistake of my answer. "Yes, it is safe for me to leave with my son."

"Good, then please come with us," the guard said, reaching down to unlock my door for the last time.

After only a few steps, the guard stopped, turned and looked at me.

"Why are we stopping?" I thought to myself.

"Wait," the guard said as if suddenly changing his mind. "We can't leave yet."

My heart started thumping loud enough to be heard throughout the entire prison. I panicked. I looked at the guard, praying that he was not playing a joke on me. I was only a few feet away from my cell, but there was no way that I could go back. I was already freer than I had been in more than seven years.

"You need to collect all of your things," the guard said. "Once we leave tonight, you will not be coming back to collect your belongings."

I looked back at him and smiled. "I have everything I need," I said confidently. "Everything in that cell can be given to the other women in the prison. They will need it more than me."

"Very well," the guard replied and turned and continued walking. "Follow me," he said with his back to me. I followed the guard toward the front guard house and looked in each cell as I passed by.

As I walked by one of the cells only a few steps away from mine, a woman was on the ground sewing a dress. Her face was forlorn as she glanced up at me. She was making a dress for her execution. It would be the last dress she would ever wear.

When she looked at me, I saw her hopelessness and recognized it. Looking at her was like looking back in time when I too felt hopeless. I remember how I drew courage from Psalm 42, "'Why must I go about mourning, oppressed by the enemy?' My bones suffer mortal agony as my foes taunt me, saying to me all day long, 'Where is your God?' Why, my soul, are you downcast? Why so disturbed within me? Put your hope in God, for I will yet praise him, my Savior and my God" (Psalm 42:9–11 NIV).

I walked out of the Multan Women's Prison just as the evening sun was going down. With the prison behind me, I could see the outline of what seemed to be my grown children in front of me. I wanted to run to them and take them into my arms, but I had to walk with the guards. As soon as I had them in my arms, I didn't want to let them go.

That evening we were taken to a military compound and given a villa to live in. The villa was surrounded by military guards to provide protection. Shafqat was also released from prison and brought to the villa where we were once again reunited. The villa had several floors with rooms for each of the children, but we all slept in the same room and in the same bed. Being with my children again was like heaven. I didn't want to let them go.

We had to stay at the villa until passports could be arranged for us to depart Pakistan. It was no longer safe for us to live in the nation of our birth. A nation in the European Union sent representatives to work on our travel documents, and they worked with us to help us to relocate our family to a safe place.

In order to get our travel documents from the Pakistan government, the entire passport office had to be shut down and all the workers had to be gone. "If the locals working at the passport office learn that you are applying for a passport, they will no doubt be angered," one of the Pakistani officials told us. "So, the entire building will be emptied before your passport will be issued."

It felt so odd that nations across the world in Europe were willing to accept our family, but our own nation of Pakistan wanted us dead. We didn't speak any European languages. Our culture was not European. We didn't have any connections to Europe, yet they were welcoming us with open arms to help save our lives.

After spending a month at the military safe house, our little family was secretly taken to the international airport in Islamabad. Our driver took us to a small door on the side of the airport so that no one could see us. Military guards on every side of us took us into the airport and then out onto the tarmac where a small plane waited on us to fly out to our new home in Europe.

Before walking up the stairs onto the small plane, I stopped and silently prayed to God. I knew that my feet would be leaving Pakistani soil for the last time. I had never been outside of

Pakistan and didn't know what to expect. Some departures are mundane while others are unforgettable, but few are forever.

Overcome with emotions, I silently said my farewell. I had dreamed of this moment of freedom every day in prison and now that it was finally here, I was deeply saddened. The nation that I loved didn't love me in return, but I didn't want to leave like this. I didn't want to leave with hate and bitterness. Christ took all that away. I didn't hold any hate in my heart for those who had falsely accused me or sentenced me to death. I have nothing but love for the nation of Pakistan.

"Do not remember me as an enemy, Pakistan, because I never hated you. Remember me as I am. Remember me as family. I will always be the little girl left in awe at your majestic mountains, colorful landscapes, and forested deserts. I will carry you with me forever and always be saddened that I was forced to leave."

I looked up to heaven as I boarded the flight. "Lord, You broke all the chains. I am finally free. You fulfilled every promise and turned my tears into laughter and my pain to joy."

31

THE ONGOING FIGHT FOR THE FAITHFUL

After settling down with my family in Europe, I have seen my children learn a new language and adapt to a new culture. My husband Shafqat has received medical treatment and care and during the writing of this book, he was being issued a state-of-the-art wheelchair by the government healthcare system.

Our life is much safer in Europe, but I still must hide my identity. I cannot share the details of where I live because there are Muslims from Pakistan that have vowed to hunt me down and carry out the death sentence that they feel that I have escaped.

Though I keep a low profile, I refuse to remain silent. I believe that God has allowed me to live to be a voice for the voiceless and to be an advocate for other Christians who are currently suffering from persecution.

Since I was released from prison, I have spoken in several government forums to share about the plight of believers who suffer from blasphemy laws. The situation has not gotten better in Pakistan but has actually grown worse.

On January 17, 2023, Pakistan's National Assembly unanimously voted to expand the country's blasphemy laws, which carry the death penalty for insulting Islam or the Prophet Muhammad.

What is truly concerning is the rules for what constitutes an insult to Islam or the Prophet Muhammad can be almost anything, and all it really takes is an accusation. In the past three decades, approximately 1,500 Pakistanis have been charged with blasphemy. Since 1990, more than seventy people have been dragged into the streets and murdered by angry mobs when Muslim clerics believed that the police were not carrying out justice fast enough.

In February 2023, a mob in eastern Pakistan stormed a police station, pulled a man accused of blasphemy from his cell in front of the police, dragged him out of the jail in broad daylight, lynched him in the streets and burned his body. Several Pakistani children participated in the brutal lynching.

Another incident took place in August 2023, when a Christian was accused of blasphemy, and at least five churches were attacked, with videos shared on social media showing mobs raiding Christian houses of worship, tearing down crosses, and setting them on fire. The police were helpless to stop the violence.

As I finished writing this book, a young Christian couple, Shaukat Masih and his wife Kiran, from my home province of Punjab, were arrested on charges of blasphemy. They have been accused of desecrating the Qur'an even though there is no real evidence. If convicted, they will be sentenced to death.

The real problem is blasphemy laws are popular among most Muslim countries; however, these laws are not just restricted to Muslim nations. As of September 2023, ninety-five countries have legislation criminalizing blasphemy.[6]

In July 2023, prompted by free speech laws in Sweden, the United Nations General Assembly voted on a Pakistani co-sponsored resolution, to make "hate speech" a prosecutable offense. Hate speech is often used as an alternative term for blasphemy in international forums but is the same thing. Muslim leaders from the fifty-seven nation Organization of Islamic Cooperation (OIC) demanded that European nations prevent and prosecute such anti-Islamic acts.

Pakistan's Mission Counsellor Bilal Chaudhry said that the resolution was a landmark point to condemn all "premeditated acts that have desecrated the Qur'an" and he called for nations to adopt laws that punish those responsible for acts of blasphemy. "Islamophobia is on the rise, with the repeated incidents of desecration of the Holy Qur'an," Chaudhry said. "Such incidents are also a manifestation of racial hatred and xenophobia, and absence of preventive legal deterrence, inaction, and shying away from speaking out encourages further incitement to hatred and violence."[7]

---

6. Luke Wilson, "Legislation Factsheet: Blasphemy (2023 Update)," United States Commission on International Religious Freedom, September 2023, https://www.uscirf.gov/publications/legislation-factsheet-blasphemy-laws.
7. Arab News Pakistan, "UN adopts Pakistan-backed resolution condemning desecration of religious symbols, holy books," *Arab News,* July 26, 2023, https://www.arabnews.com/node/2344536/pakistan.

The laws are pushed in the name of stopping hate, promoting tolerance, and interreligious respect, but the truth is that the same OIC nations promoting the bill put Christians on death row for refusing to abandon their faith.

On September 6, 2023, I traveled to the European Union and spoke about the danger of blasphemy laws shrouded in "anti-hate" speech language. There is no freedom found in anti-blasphemy laws no matter how wonderfully they are packaged.

I had to leave my home of birth because of the intolerance for my Christian faith and I have found refuge in Europe. It is not just Christians who suffer from these laws. During my time in Europe, I often found myself living among people of many different faiths, including Muslims, who have also had to flee their Islamic homelands due to blasphemy laws.

Every day I wake up thinking of persecuted believers who sit in prisons because of their faith. There are so many underrepresented, disadvantaged, and vulnerable followers of Christ that are invisible to the rest of the world that I feel called to make visible.

The words of Hebrews 13:3 commands us, "*Remember them that are in bonds, as bound with them*" (KJV)."

I am too grateful to God for releasing me from prison to not remember the estimated three hundred million Christians worldwide who are denied basic human rights because of their faith in Jesus Christ.

ABOUT THE AUTHORS

SHAGUFTA KAUSAR

Raised as a Christian minority in a Muslim nation, Shagufta Kausar learned early on to never argue about faith or to stand up for her beliefs. Doing so could easily lead to riots and deadly violence, so she was told to always be silent, like a lamb.

In 2013, local police raided Shagufta's home, accusing her of sending a blasphemous text to a local imam. As a mother of four, Shagufta was arrested, her handicapped husband, Shafqat, was hung upside down and beaten, and her children were put in state custody. The truth was, Shagufta didn't even have a phone and was illiterate—she couldn't write or speak the language in the text. She was impossibly innocent.

Convicted at a trial she was not allowed to attend and sentenced to death by hanging, Shagufta was told that she could save herself and her family if she would only abandon her faith and accept Islam. Under threat of death, she refused.

Her stunning true story of a courageous mother of four standing against the tyranny of her country's blasphemy laws illuminates the reality of what many Christians around the world face every day. Shagufta is a voice for Christian minorities who suffer daily persecution under unjust laws.

EUGENE BACH

Eugene Bach is a pseudonym for a member of the Chinese underground church who, for security reasons, does not wish to be identified. He has been working with the underground church in China for twenty years, helping to establish forward missions bases in closed countries around the world, including Iraq and Syria. Eugene leads the Chinese missionary movement Back to Jerusalem, which provides essential support for Chinese missionaries in Africa, Asia, and the Middle East, and he has written books about the underground church in China, North Korea, and Iran. His books with Whitaker House include *China and End-Time Prophecy; I Didn't Survive; I Stand with Christ; ISIS: The Heart of Terror; Kidnapped by a Cult; Leaving Buddha; Shackled Smuggling Light;* and *The Underground Church.*